Developmental Exercises for
The Bedford Handbook

Ninth Edition

Wanda Van Goor

formerly of Prince George's Community College

Diana Hacker

Bedford / St. Martin's

Boston ◆ New York

For information, write: Bedford/St. Martin's
75 Arlington Street, Boston, MA 02116
(617) 399-4000

ISBN 978-1-4576-5078-9

Preface for Instructors

The exercises in this book are specifically designed for developmental students. All have been classroom tested.

The exercises in each set are thematically linked, usually focusing on the achievements of a famous person or group—such as John Muir, Louis Braille, impressionist painters, Amelia Earhart, Jackie Robinson, or the Beatles—so that students are reading real prose on interesting topics rather than unrelated drill sentences.

Here are the principal features of *Developmental Exercises for The Bedford Handbook*, Ninth Edition.

Respectful of students' college status

Although the exercises vary in level of difficulty, all of them respect the age and experience of college students. Most exercises ask students to edit paragraphs and essays, not to fill in blanks or recopy whole sentences when only a word or two may need changing. Where possible, exercises encourage students to think about the impact of errors on readers and to choose revision strategies that produce effective, not just "correct," writing.

Written in connected discourse

Because nearly every exercise is a paragraph, an essay, or a set of numbered sentences that are connected in meaning, students learn to identify and revise problem sentences in realistic contexts. These connected discourse exercises mimic the process of revision as it occurs in real writing. In addition, they provide a rhetorical context to guide students as they select among revision strategies. When revising comma splices and fused sentences, for example, students will see that relying too heavily on the period and the semicolon results in dull, monotonous prose. They will begin to see the need for occasional subordination, and the rhetorical context will suggest just where subordination would be most effective.

"Guided practice" exercises

Most sections open with a guided practice exercise that gives students special help. Section codes (such as 21, 21c) in the margin identify problem sentences and tell students where in *The Bedford Handbook*, Ninth Edition, to look for explanations and revision strategies. Answers to these exercises appear in the back of the book.

Varied formats

Seldom will students be asked to do exactly the same thing in two consecutive exercises. Varied ways of working on a topic keep the task interesting. Sometimes students need only to circle the letter of the correct or clearer sentence in a pair of sentences; sometimes they choose between two words or phrases; frequently they edit, crossing out incorrect or confusing forms and adding handwritten revisions; occasionally they edit the same sentence in two different ways.

Many exercises provide hints for students, telling them, for example, that two of the ten sentences in a set are correct or that half of the sentences use a strategy, such as parallelism, correctly and the other half need revision.

Emphasis on reading

As they learn to edit the sentences and paragraphs in the exercises, students do a considerable amount of reading, and many exercises ask them to respond as readers. In an exercise on mixed constructions, for example, students are asked to discriminate between the easy-to-read and the hard-to-read sentences. Where possible, students are encouraged to think about meaning. "Which sentences are unclear?" an exercise on needed words asks. An exercise on adjectives and adverbs asks what the difference is between the sentences "Most slaves did not find their escape routes easy" and "Most slaves did not find their escape routes easily."

Cross-curricular content

Most exercises profile a person or group that students are likely to encounter in college courses across the curriculum: Mary Wollstonecraft, Albert Einstein, Martin Luther King Jr., Sacagawea, Mother Jones, and so on. Because many of these people overcame great obstacles to achieve their goals, their stories are often inspirational as well as informative.

Adaptable to a variety of teaching styles

You can use the exercises in a variety of ways. Instructors have used them successfully for homework or quizzes, for nongraded individual study, for class discussions, and for collaborative learning in small groups.

Acknowledgments

I am grateful to several people at Bedford/St. Martin's who were actively involved in the book's development and production. Executive editor Michelle Clark has offered intelligent suggestions and upbeat encouragement, and senior editor Barbara Flanagan has reworked the exercises through several editions. Associate editor Kylie Paul oversaw the development of this edition. Julie Nichols and Christy Stillwell provided several new exercises on contemporary themes. Production editor Lidia MacDonald-Carr guided our complex manuscript through production.

Thanks also go to Claire Seng-Niemoeller for designing the book's pages and to copyeditor Leslie Connor for bringing consistency and clarity to the final manuscript.

Finally, since Diana Hacker will always be a part of my work on the exercises, I'd like to echo her words: "For their support and encouragement, we would like to thank our families, our colleagues at Prince George's Community College, and the many students over the years who have taught us that errors, a natural by-product of the writing process, are simply problems waiting to be solved."

Wanda Van Goor
formerly of Prince George's Community College

Introduction for Students

To learn any skill—whether snowboarding, tennis, CPR, Web design, or the electric guitar—takes practice. Writing well is no exception: In a college composition class, you will learn to write by writing, and you will learn to revise by revising.

Developmental Exercises for The Bedford Handbook, Ninth Edition, will sharpen your revision skills by giving you a great deal of controlled, yet realistic, practice. Let's say, for example, that you want to learn to identify and revise sentence fragments. Your first step is to read section 19 in *The Bedford Handbook*, Ninth Edition, and to study the flowchart on page 279. Then, keeping *The Bedford Handbook* open to section 19, work on Exercise 19-1 in *Developmental Exercises for The Bedford Handbook*. Exercise 19-1, a "guided practice," gives codes in the margin (such as 19a or 19c) next to any word group that is a fragment. In addition to alerting you where to look for fragments, the codes refer to specific rules in the text; if you have trouble identifying or fixing a particular fragment, you can consult *The Bedford Handbook* for help. When you have finished the exercise, you should check your answers. Answers to the guided practice exercises appear in the back of this book, beginning on page 187.

Once you have done the guided practice exercise, attempt the other exercises in the set; continue to refer to *The Bedford Handbook* when you run into trouble. You'll find that the rest of the exercises in a set vary in style and level of difficulty. In the set on fragments, for example, one exercise asks you to identify the complete sentence in a pair of word groups; another, presented in paragraph form, asks you to identify fragments and to think about possible revision strategies; and three other exercises give you practice in both identifying and revising fragments. Throughout the entire set of exercises, the subject you'll be reading about is the Beatles. Other exercise sets resemble the one on fragments. In those sets you will encounter a number of famous people you are likely to read about in other college classes: men and women such as Karl Marx, John Muir, Frederick Douglass, Albert Einstein, impressionist painters, and Amelia Earhart.

Wanda Van Goor
formerly of Prince George's Community College

Contents

Preface for Instructors   iii

Acknowledgments   v

Introduction for Students   vi

Clear sentences

8-1	Active verbs: Guided practice	1
8-2	Active verbs	2
8-3	Active verbs	3
8-4	Active verbs: Guided review	4
9-1	Parallelism: Guided practice	5
9-2	Parallelism	6
9-3	Parallelism	7
9-4	Parallelism: Guided review	8
10-1	Needed words: Guided practice	9
10-2	Needed words	10
10-3	Needed words	11
10-4	Needed words: Guided review	12
11-1	Mixed constructions: Guided practice	13
11-2	Mixed constructions	14
11-3	Mixed constructions	15
11-4	Mixed constructions: Guided review	16
12-1	Misplaced and dangling modifiers: Guided practice	17
12-2	Misplaced modifiers	18
12-3	Misplaced and dangling modifiers	19
12-4	Misplaced and dangling modifiers: Guided review	20
13-1	Distracting shifts: Guided practice	21
13-2	Distracting shifts	22
13-3	Distracting shifts	23
13-4	Distracting shifts: Guided review	24
14-1	Emphasis: Guided practice	25
14-2	Emphasis	26
14-3	Emphasis	27
14-4	Emphasis: Guided review	28
15-1	Variety: Guided practice	29
15-2	Variety	30
15-3	Variety: Guided review	31

Review of 8–15: Clear sentences   32

Word choice

16-1	Wordy sentences: Guided practice	33
16-2	Wordy sentences	34
16-3	Wordy sentences	35
16-4	Wordy sentences: Guided review	37
17-1	Appropriate language: Guided practice	38
17-2	Appropriate language	39
17-3	Appropriate language	41
17-4	Appropriate language: Guided review	42
18-1	Exact words: Guided practice	43
18-2	Exact words	44
18-3	Exact words	45
18-4	Exact words	46
18-5	Exact words: Guided review	47

Review of 16–18: Word choice   49

Grammatical sentences

19-1	Fragments: Guided practice	51
19-2	Fragments	52
19-3	Fragments	53
19-4	Fragments	54
19-5	Fragments	55
19-6	Fragments: Guided review	56
20-1	Run-on sentences: Guided practice	57
20-2	Run-on sentences	59
20-3	Run-on sentences	61
20-4	Run-on sentences	62
20-5	Run-on sentences: Guided review	63
21-1	Subject-verb agreement: Guided practice	64
21-2	Subject-verb agreement	65
21-3	Subject-verb agreement	66
21-4	Subject-verb agreement: Guided review	67
22-1	Pronoun-antecedent agreement: Guided practice	68
22-2	Pronoun-antecedent agreement	69
22-3	Pronoun-antecedent agreement	70
22-4	Pronoun-antecedent agreement: Guided review	71
23-1	Pronoun reference: Guided practice	72
23-2	Pronoun reference	73
23-3	Pronoun reference	74
23-4	Pronoun reference: Guided review	75
24-1	Pronoun and noun case: Guided practice	76
24-2	Pronoun and noun case	77
24-3	Pronoun and noun case	78
24-4	Pronoun and noun case: Guided review	79
25-1	*Who* and *whom*: Guided practice	80
25-2	*Who* and *whom*	81
25-3	*Who* and *whom*	82

25-4	*Who* and *whom*: Guided review	83
26-1	Adjectives and adverbs: Guided practice	84
26-2	Adjectives and adverbs	85
26-3	Adjectives and adverbs	86
26-4	Adjectives and adverbs: Guided review	87
27-1	Verb forms: Guided practice	88
27-2	Verb forms	89
27-3	Verb forms	90
27-4	Verb forms: Guided review	91
27-5	Verb tense and mood: Guided practice	92
27-6	Verb tense and mood	93
27-7	Verb tense and mood	94
27-8	Verb tense and mood: Guided review	95

Review of 19–27: Grammatical sentences — 96

Multilingual writers and ESL challenges

28-1	ESL verb use: Guided practice	97
28-2	Verb forms	98
28-3	Helping verbs, main verbs, and omitted verbs	99
28-4	Verb forms	100
28-5	Passive verbs	101
28-6	Conditional verbs	102
28-7	Verbs followed by gerunds or infinitives	103
28-8	Verbs followed by gerunds or infinitives	104
28-9	ESL verb use: Guided review	105
29-1	Articles: Guided practice	106
29-2	Articles	107
29-3	Articles	108
29-4	Articles: Guided review	109
30/31-1	Sentence structure, prepositions, and idiomatic expressions: Guided practice	110
30/31-2	Omissions and needless repetitions	111
30/31-3	Present and past participles	112
30/31-4	Placement of adjectives	113
30/31-5	Sentence structure, prepositions, and idiomatic expressions: Guided review	115

Review of 28–31: Multilingual writers and ESL challenges — 117

Punctuation

32/33-1	The comma and unnecessary commas: Guided practice	118
32/33-2	The comma	119
32/33-3	The comma	121
32/33-4	The comma	123
32/33-5	Unnecessary commas	124

32/33-6	Unnecessary commas	125
32/33-7	The comma and unnecessary commas: Guided review	126
34-1	The semicolon: Guided practice	127
34-2	The semicolon	128
34-3	The semicolon	129
34-4	The semicolon: Guided review	130
35-1	The colon: Guided practice	131
35-2	The colon	132
35-3	The colon	133
35-4	The colon: Guided review	134
36-1	The apostrophe: Guided practice	135
36-2	The apostrophe	136
36-3	The apostrophe	137
36-4	The apostrophe: Guided review	138
37-1	Quotation marks: Guided practice	139
37-2	Quotation marks	140
37-3	Quotation marks	141
37-4	Quotation marks: Guided review	142
38-1	End punctuation: Guided practice	143
38-2	End punctuation	144
38-3	End punctuation: Guided review	145
39-1	Other punctuation marks: Guided practice	148
39-2	Other punctuation marks	149
39-3	Other punctuation marks	150
39-4	Other punctuation marks: Guided review	151

Review of 32–39: Punctuation   152

Mechanics

40/41/42-1	Abbreviations, numbers, and italics: Guided practice	153
40/41/42-2	Abbreviations and numbers	154
40/41/42-3	Italics	155
40/41/42-4	Abbreviations, numbers, and italics: Guided review	156
43/44/45-1	Spelling, the hyphen, and capitalization: Guided practice	157
43/44/45-2	Spelling	158
43/44/45-3	The hyphen	159
43/44/45-4	Capitalization	160
43/44/45-5	Spelling, the hyphen, and capitalization: Guided review	161

Review of 40–45: Mechanics   162

Grammar basics

46-1	Parts of speech: Preview	163
46-2	Nouns and noun/adjectives	164
46-3	Nouns and noun/adjectives	165
46-4	Pronouns and pronoun/adjectives	166

46-5	Verbs	167
46-6	Adjectives and adverbs	168
46-7	Prepositions	169
46-8	Prepositions and conjunctions	170
46-9	Parts of speech: Review	171
47-1	Sentence patterns: Preview	172
47-2	Subjects	173
47-3	Direct objects and subject complements	174
47-4	Indirect objects and object complements	175
47-5	Direct objects, indirect objects, and object complements	176
47-6	Sentence patterns: Review	177
48-1	Subordinate word groups: Preview	178
48-2	Prepositional phrases	179
48-3	Prepositional and verbal phrases	180
48-4	Verbal phrases	181
48-5	Subordinate clauses	182
48-6	Subordinate word groups: Review	183
49-1	Sentence types: Preview	184
49-2	Sentence types	185
49-3	Sentence types: Review	186

Answers to Guided Practice and Preview Exercises 187

EXERCISE 8-1 ◆ Active verbs: Guided practice

Revise any weak or unemphatic sentences by replacing passive verbs or *be* verbs with active alternatives. The numbers in the margin refer to relevant rules in section 8 of *The Bedford Handbook*, Ninth Edition. The first revision has been done for you; a suggested revision of this exercise appears in the back of this book.

Young slave Frederick Douglass enjoyed indulging

~~Indulging~~ in his favorite fantasy about slave owners. ~~was something that young~~   8b

~~slave Frederick Douglass enjoyed.~~ In his fantasy, everyone was in a conspiracy against   8b

the slave owners. No hint of a planned escape was given by slaves still in bondage.   8a

Members of the community never revealed the whereabouts of escaped slaves. Slaves

who escaped successfully never talked too much about how they got away. Owners

were told nothing at all by slaves they recaptured. Even some white southerners who   8a

sympathized with the slaves gave no information to their slave-owning friends. The

part of his fantasy that Douglass enjoyed most was the final part. In it, Douglass   8b

imagined slave owners as being too afraid to hunt escaping slaves. The owners were   8b

distrustful of their slaves, their enemies, and even their friends.

EXERCISE 8-2 ◆ Active verbs

To read about this topic, see section 8 in *The Bedford Handbook*, Ninth Edition.

In the following paired sentences, circle the letter of the sentence in which the verbs are active and emphatic. Be ready to explain your choice. Example:

    a. **On his second attempt, Frederick was able to escape by pretending to be a sailor.**

    (b.) **On his second attempt, Frederick escaped slavery by pretending to be a sailor.**

1. a. The use of another man's sailing papers was the way Frederick got to Philadelphia.

   b. Frederick used another man's sailing papers to get to Philadelphia.

2. a. He did not even consider the possibility of staying in Philadelphia.

   b. The possibility of staying in Philadelphia was not even considered by him.

3. a. In Philadelphia, he asked the first black man he saw how to get to New York.

   b. In Philadelphia, the first black man he saw was asked how to get to New York.

4. a. Arriving in New York was what made Frederick feel safe.

   b. Arriving in New York made Frederick feel safe.

5. a. Luckily, a sympathetic abolitionist found Frederick before a slave catcher could find him.

   b. Luckily, Frederick was found by a sympathetic abolitionist before a slave catcher could find him.

Van Goor and Hacker, *Developmental Exercises for The Bedford Handbook*, 9th ed. (Boston: Bedford, 2014)

EXERCISE 8-3 ◆ Active verbs

To read about this topic, see section 8 in *The Bedford Handbook*, Ninth Edition.

Half of the following sentences contain passive verbs or verbs that are a form of *be*. Find them and change them to active verbs. You may need to invent a subject for some verbs, and you may need to make major revisions in some sentences. If a sentence already contains only active verbs, mark it as "active." Example:

P

~~Frederick Douglass was annoyed by~~ ₱eople who spoke openly of helping the underground

annoyed Frederick Douglass.

railroad/

1. Douglass said that by talking openly about it, these people had turned the "underground railroad" into an "upperground railroad."

2. Although these people were deserving of praise, their open talk endangered escaping slaves.

3. Such talk alerted slave owners to possible escape routes.

4. Escaping slaves would often be caught by professional slave hunters at the houses of those who talked openly.

5. All slaves were threatened by any information that increased slave owners' knowledge.

6. Whenever slave owners suspected some of the escape routes, the courage of the slaves was lost.

7. Frederick Douglass understood the slaves' fears very well: His first attempt to escape had failed.

8. Professional slave breakers beat and tortured captured slaves until the slaves submitted or died.

9. His own treatment at the hands of slave breakers left Douglass with severe, disfiguring scars all over his back.

10. Years later, northerners were convinced by those scars that Douglass spoke the truth about slavery.

Van Goor and Hacker, *Developmental Exercises for*
The Bedford Handbook, 9th ed. (Boston: Bedford, 2014)

8-3 | Active verbs **3**

EXERCISE 8-4 ◆ Active verbs: Guided review

Revise any weak or unemphatic sentences by replacing passive verbs or *be* verbs with active verbs. The numbers in the margin refer to relevant rules in section 8 of *The Bedford Handbook*, Ninth Edition. The first revision has been done for you.

      ~~Some of~~ Frederick Douglass *changed some of his* ideas about the North ~~were changed~~ after his   8a

successful escape from slavery. Before that time, Douglass's assumption was that   8b

northerners lacked both money and culture. In the South, only poor people owned

no slaves. Also, no lovely homes, no pianos, no art, and often no books were owned by   8a

poor people. When he first saw New Bedford, Massachusetts, Douglass was doubtful of   8b

his own eyesight. He saw no dilapidated houses or naked children or barefoot women

in New Bedford. Instead, the beautiful homes with equally beautiful furniture and

gardens were an indication of considerable wealth. Quality merchandise was handled   8b, 8a

by laborers on the wharves and purchased by them in the stores. When he saw all of

this, Douglass happily changed his ideas about the North.

Van Goor and Hacker, *Developmental Exercises for The Bedford Handbook*, 9th ed. (Boston: Bedford, 2014)

EXERCISE 9-1 ◆ Parallelism: Guided practice

Edit the following paragraphs to correct faulty parallelism. The numbers in the margin refer to relevant rules in section 9 of *The Bedford Handbook*, Ninth Edition. The first revision has been done for you; a suggested revision of this exercise appears in the back of this book.

In his own time, one famous sixteenth-century Italian was known only by his given name, Leonardo. Today he is still known by that single name. But then and now, his name suggests many different roles: biologist, botanist, inventor, engineer, strategist, researcher, and artist.

Sixteenth-century Venetian soldiers knew Leonardo as a military strategist. When the Turkish fleet was invading their country, Leonardo suggested conducting surprise underwater attacks and ~~to flood~~ *flooding* the land that the Turkish army had to   9b
cross. Engineers knew him as the man who laid out new canals for the city of Milan. Scientists admired him for not only his precise anatomical drawings but also for his   9b
discovery that hardening of the arteries could cause death. To Milan's royal court, Leonardo was the artist who was painting impressive portraits, sculpting a bronze horse memorial to the house of Sforza, and at the same time worked on a mural of the   9a
Last Supper.

Leonardo saw a three-dimensional *s*-curve in all of nature—the flow of water, the movements of animals, and how birds flew. We recognize the same *s*-curve today   9a
in the spiraling form of DNA. Leonardo invented the wave theory: He saw that grain bending as the wind blew over it and water rippling from a stone dropped into it were the same scientific event. It was as easy for him to see this wave in sound and light as observing it in fields and streams. The math of his day could not explain all his   9b
theories, but twentieth-century scientists showed the world that Leonardo knew what he was talking about.

Leonardo saw very clearly that the powers of nature could be destructive and human beings could be savage. At the same time, he saw a unity holding all of life's   9c
varied parts together, a unity he could express in his art.

Leonardo—it's quite a name!

Van Goor and Hacker, *Developmental Exercises for The Bedford Handbook*, 9th ed. (Boston: Bedford, 2014)

9-1 | Parallelism: Guided practice   **5**

EXERCISE 9-2 ◆ Parallelism

To read about this topic, see section 9 in *The Bedford Handbook*, Ninth Edition.

All of the following sentences make an attempt to use parallel structure. Half of them succeed. The other five need revision. Put "OK" by the correct ones, and edit the other five to correct faulty parallelism. Example:

> **Leonardo spent the first years of his life playing in the fields, drawing animals and plants,**
> *building*
> **and ~~he built~~ miniature bridges and towers along the river.**
>   ^

1. When Leonardo moved to Florence to live with his father, he exchanged a slow-moving rural life for a fast-paced urban one.

2. Because his birth parents had not been married, many job opportunities were not available to Leonardo. He could not become a merchant, a banker, or a skilled craftsman.

3. It was no easier for Leonardo to attend the local university than learning a craft.

4. The obvious choices were to become a soldier or he could join the priesthood.

5. Leonardo did not want his future to be in either the church or the army.

6. Deciding that Leonardo could draw better than he could march or pray, his father placed him with a major artist, Andrea del Verrocchio.

7. Verrocchio's shop worked for all kinds of customers, including trade unions, churches, and they would work for individuals also.

8. Living in Verrocchio's home and working in his shop, Leonardo heard talk of new theories about geography and science while he learned skills like modeling, painting, and sculpture.

9. Perhaps even more important was the variety of instruments Leonardo learned to make, among them musical, navigational, and ones for surgeons to use.

10. Working with Verrocchio was like going to three schools: an art school, a technology institute, and a liberal arts college.

Van Goor and Hacker, *Developmental Exercises for*
The Bedford Handbook, 9th ed. (Boston: Bedford, 2014)

EXERCISE 9-3 ◆ Parallelism

To read about this topic, see section 9 in *The Bedford Handbook*, Ninth Edition.

Circle the letter of the word or word group that best completes the parallel structure in each sentence. Example:

Leonardo was handsome, generous, clever, and _____.

a. **ambidextrous**

b. **able to use either hand for most activities**

c. **he could use either hand for most activities**

1. Leonardo's life had three distinct periods: his childhood in Vinci, his apprenticeship in

   Florence, and _____ .

   a. when he was an adult

   b. his being an adult and earning his own way

   c. his adulthood in various Italian cities

2. In childhood, Leonardo had not only a loving family and relatives but also _____ .

   a. safe and unspoiled acres to explore

   b. he had the whole gentle slope of a mountain to explore

   c. including fields and vineyards to explore

3. However, two natural events haunted his memory for years: A hurricane destroyed much of

   the valley below his village, and _____ .

   a. a flood washed away much of the city of Florence

   b. a flood that washed away much of the city of Florence

   c. the boiling, muddy, surging waters of a flood

4. Wind and water became major topics for Leonardo's study. He decided that wind and water

   were both useful and _____ .

   a. did harmful things

   b. they caused harm

   c. harmful

5. Viewers can find in many of Leonardo's works small round pebbles washed by a stream,

   riverbanks covered with moss and flowers, and _____ .

   a. little freshwater crabs partly hidden beneath rocks

   b. viewers can find small freshwater crabs under rocks

   c. little freshwater crabs sometimes hide beneath rocks

Van Goor and Hacker, *Developmental Exercises for The Bedford Handbook*, 9th ed. (Boston: Bedford, 2014)

9-3 | Parallelism　**7**

EXERCISE 9-4 ◆ Parallelism: Guided review

Edit the following paragraphs to correct faulty parallelism. The numbers in the margin refer to relevant rules in section 9 of *The Bedford Handbook*, Ninth Edition. The first revision has been done for you.

Leonardo's vision of life as one borderless unity affected both his personal life and ~~it affected~~ his artistic work. **9b**

Leonardo did not simply look at the world; he studied it carefully. Watching the wind ripple the water in a pond, he was observant, intent, and in a serious mood. **9a** Leonardo saw no boundaries in nature; to him, people and animals were parts of one creation. He ate no meat because he did not want to bring death to a fellow creature; he bought caged songbirds so that he could set them free. Having no family of his own, he adopted a boy from another family to be both his son and he would be his heir. **9b** Even right- and left-handedness were the same to him. He filled his notebooks with mirror writing, but he wrote letters, reports, and proposals in the usual way. When his right hand became crippled, he used his left.

Leonardo's view of all of life as one creation led him to artistic innovations. Before Leonardo, artists had always used outlines to separate a painting's subject from its background. Because Leonardo saw everything in nature as interrelated, he decided that using shadow and gradation of light and color was better than to use **9b** an outline. He wanted one thing to flow into another the way smoke flows into air. Looking at Mona Lisa's hand, for instance, viewers can find no line where one finger ends and the next one begins; the separation is done totally with shadows. This unified vision of the world affected the content of his paintings as well as the technique. Background and subject often echo each other in a picture: The drapery and folds of the subject's clothing may reflect background scenes of curving vines or rocky hills or water that flows. **9a**

Leonardo recognized the great diversity surrounding him, but he believed that an even greater unity supported the diversity and his own work was an expression of **9c** that unity.

Van Goor and Hacker, *Developmental Exercises for The Bedford Handbook*, 9th ed. (Boston: Bedford, 2014)

Name _____ Section _____ Date _____

EXERCISE 10-1 ◆ Needed words: Guided practice

Add any words needed for grammatical or logical completeness in the following paragraphs. The numbers in the margin refer to relevant rules in section 10 of *The Bedford Handbook*, Ninth Edition. The first revision has been done for you; a suggested revision of this exercise appears in the back of this book.

Mary Wollstonecraft, an eighteenth-century writer, may have been England's first feminist. Her entire life reflected her belief in equal rights for women in all areas of their lives: personal, intellectual, and professional.

accepted
From childhood, she never had and never would accept the idea that men were superior to women. As a young girl, she knew that her drinking and gambling father deserved less respect than her long-suffering mother did. As an adult, she demanded that society give her the same freedom it gave men.

10a

Wollstonecraft also demanded men pay attention to her ideas. She did not argue about an idea. Instead, she gave an example of what she objected to and invited her readers to think about it from various points of view. Working this way, she made few enemies among intellectuals. Indeed, she was attracted and respected by some of the leading intellectuals of her day. Among them she was as well known on one side of the Atlantic as on the other. Thomas Paine, the American orator and writer, probably knew her better than Samuel Johnson, the English writer.

10b

10a

10c

Professionally, she was a governess, teacher, and author. When her father's drinking destroyed the family, she and her sisters started a girls' school. Eventually, financial problems forced the school to close, but not before Mary had acquired enough firsthand experience to write *Thoughts on the Education of Daughters* (1786). As competent or more competent than other writers of the day, she was a more persuasive advocate for women than most other writers were.

10d

10c

Modern feminists may find it ironic that current encyclopedia entries for "Wollstonecraft" refer researchers to "Godwin," her married name—where they will find her entry longer than the entry for her famous husband, William Godwin.

Van Goor and Hacker, *Developmental Exercises for The Bedford Handbook*, 9th ed. (Boston: Bedford, 2014)

10-1 | Needed words: Guided practice **9**

EXERCISE 10-2 ◆ Needed words

To read about this topic, see section 10 in *The Bedford Handbook*, Ninth Edition.

Circle the letter of the clearer sentence in each pair—the sentence that contains all words needed for logical or grammatical completeness. Example:

    a.   **Mary Wollstonecraft felt a woman did not have to marry a man in order to live with him.**

    (b.)   **Mary Wollstonecraft felt that a woman did not have to marry a man in order to live with him.**

1.   a.   She never married, or wanted to, her first suitor.

        b.   She never married, or wanted to marry, her first suitor.

2.   a.   With Gilbert Imlay, she discovered that travel could teach her much about the business world.

        b.   With Gilbert Imlay, she discovered travel could teach her much about the business world.

3.   a.   She had a more intellectual relationship with William Godwin than Gilbert Imlay.

        b.   She had a more intellectual relationship with William Godwin than with Gilbert Imlay.

4.   a.   In one way, she may have been as conservative as, if not more conservative than, other women of her day.

        b.   In one way, she may have been as conservative, if not more conservative, than other women of her day.

5.   a.   Marrying Godwin when she became pregnant may have shown that she believed in and acted by society's rules for pregnant women.

        b.   Marrying Godwin when she became pregnant may have shown that she believed and acted by society's rules for pregnant women.

Van Goor and Hacker, *Developmental Exercises for The Bedford Handbook*, 9th ed. (Boston: Bedford, 2014)

EXERCISE 10-3 ◆ Needed words

To read about this topic, see section 10 in *The Bedford Handbook*, Ninth Edition.

Missing words make some of the following sentences unclear. Add the needed words so that only one meaning is possible. If a sentence is clear as written, mark it "OK." Example:

> *did.*
> **Mary Wollstonecraft approved of the French Revolution more than Edmund Burke∕**
> ^

1. Wollstonecraft blamed women's problems on the structure of society more than the men of her time.

2. Her ideas about women frightened other people less than her husband.

3. One of her daughters, Mary Shelley, who wrote *Frankenstein*, became as famous as Wollstonecraft herself.

4. The readers Mary Shelley attracted were different from those who enjoyed her mother's work.

5. Modern readers know Mary Shelley better than Mary Wollstonecraft.

Van Goor and Hacker, *Developmental Exercises for*
The Bedford Handbook, 9th ed. (Boston: Bedford, 2014)

10-3 | Needed words   **11**

EXERCISE 10-4 ◆ Needed words: Guided review

Add any words needed for grammatical or logical completeness in the following paragraphs. The numbers in the margin refer to relevant rules in section 10 of *The Bedford Handbook*, Ninth Edition. The first revision has been done for you.

          that

Most people in her era found Mary Wollstonecraft used very persuasive tech-   10b

niques. She did not argue and never had by directly attacking those who disagreed   10a

with her.

  More astute than other women of her day, she used anecdotal "observations."

She knew that a story or anecdote would make her point best. Since she did not argue,   10d

her listeners never felt they had to defend their own positions and were able to listen

to her stories with reasonably open minds. The stories, which often made clever use

of allegory and metaphor, came from her own experience and observation. Preferring

examples from dressmaking to other occupations, she chose stories that illustrated her   10c

points and let the anecdotes speak for themselves. Her technique was as convincing, or   10c

more convincing than, outright argument.

  Mary Wollstonecraft's sense of timing was also good. In 1790, she wrote a

pamphlet entitled *A Vindication of the Rights of Men*. Part of her reason for writing

it was to respond to the excitement caused by the French Revolution (1789–1799).

People liked her pamphlet very much. While enthusiasm was still high, she produced

A Vindication of the Rights of Women in 1792. It, too, was well received.

  No doubt part of Mary Wollstonecraft's unusually effective writing came from

the fact that she not only believed in but also lived the ideas she wrote about.   10a

Van Goor and Hacker, *Developmental Exercises for The Bedford Handbook*, 9th ed. (Boston: Bedford, 2014)

EXERCISE 11-1 ◆ Mixed constructions: Guided practice

Edit the following paragraphs to eliminate problems with mixed constructions. The numbers in the margin refer to relevant rules in section 11 of *The Bedford Handbook*, Ninth Edition. The first revision has been done for you; a suggested revision of this exercise appears in the back of this book.

Sometimes it's hard to separate history from folklore. Casey Jones, John Henry,

Johnny Appleseed, Uncle Sam—which of these ~~names~~ were real men? Although we've   11b

heard their stories, but are those stories true?   11a

There really was a railroad engineer called Casey Jones; the reason he got that

nickname was because of Cayce, Kentucky, where he lived as a boy. There really was   11c

a Cannonball too; it was the Illinois Central's fast mail and passenger train. There

really was a wreck of Engine No. 382, and Casey died while slowing the train to save

his passengers. Legend has it that when workers found his body in the wreckage,

his hand was still on the air-brake lever. (The use of air brakes had recently been   11b

installed on trains to increase their braking power.)

John Henry was an African American railroad worker of great strength. In

legend and song, he died after a timed contest against a steam drill. By using a

hammer in each hand made John Henry win the contest. He drilled two holes seven   11a

feet deep; the steam drill bored only one nine-foot hole. The real John Henry died on

the job, crushed by rocks that fell from the ceiling of a railroad tunnel.

John Chapman, better known as Johnny Appleseed, was a wealthy and well-

liked nurseryman who kept moving his place of business west as the frontier moved

west. His boyhood friend Sam Wilson supplied meat to the US troops during the War

of 1812. A worker told a government inspector that the "US" stamped on the meat

stood for "Uncle Sam." Although it was a joke, but it caught on, and Congress made   11a

the "Uncle Sam" identification official in the 1960s.

Van Goor and Hacker, *Developmental Exercises for*
The Bedford Handbook, 9th ed. (Boston: Bedford, 2014)

11-1 | Mixed constructions: Guided practice   **13**

EXERCISE 11-2 ◆ Mixed constructions

To read about this topic, see section 11 in *The Bedford Handbook*, Ninth Edition.

Correct the mixed constructions in the following sentences. Example:

> **What European first set eyes on America? If you say Amerigo Vespucci, from whom the**
>
> **name "America" is said to derive, ~~so~~ you'll be only half right.**

1. Although Vespucci claimed to have found a new continent, but there is no evidence that he ever reached any land in the Western Hemisphere.

2. Columbus may have seen parts of the Americas first, but when a German mapmaker believed Vespucci's claim and put Vespucci's name on the map explains why the lands became known as America.

3. If Vespucci wasn't the first European to find land across the Atlantic, so who was?

4. For most British historians who have worked on the question say that John Cabot got there first.

5. Early mariners, a very dangerous occupation, often sailed under several names.

6. John Cabot was the name for Italian mariner Giovanni Caboto used when he worked for the English.

7. Some people say that Leif Eriksson saw the coast of North America first; their reason is because he established a small community on Newfoundland about AD 1000.

8. Even though Eriksson's community was established five hundred years before the time of Vespucci, Columbus, and Cabot, but the Norse sagas claim that Bjarni Herjulfsson sighted North America before Eriksson did.

9. The growth in the number of theories increases as new evidence is found.

10. So who was the first European on American shores? As these bits of history indicate that no one can really answer that question.

Van Goor and Hacker, *Developmental Exercises for*
The Bedford Handbook, 9th ed. (Boston: Bedford, 2014)

EXERCISE 11-3 ◆ Mixed constructions

To read about this topic, see section 11 in *The Bedford Handbook*, Ninth Edition.

Read through each sentence just once. If it sounds correct to you, put "OK" after it. If it sounds like a mixed construction, put "MC" after it. Then go back and check; only four of the sentences should have "OK" after them. Fix the others. Example:

> **Do you believe that ~~because of~~ Paul Revere's late-night horseback ride alerted Minutemen from Boston to Lexington to Concord that the British were coming?** ___*MC*___

1. In college, most American students discover that their knowledge of history is a mixture of fact and fiction. _____

2. For example, most students believe that Paul Revere rode alone, alerting citizens from Boston to Concord that the British were coming. In fact, Revere did not ride alone, and he never made it to Concord. _____

3. Since he was able to borrow a horse permitted Revere to get as far as Lexington. _____

4. By adding two other riders, William Dawes and Samuel Prescott, made it possible to get the warning to Concord. _____

5. The vigilance of a group of British soldiers on patrol overtook all three men, captured Revere, and found out who he was. _____

6. The reason Minutemen reported promptly for duty was because they were warned by relays of riders who had been alerted by prearranged signals. _____

7. If Henry Wadsworth Longfellow had not written a poem about the ride forty-five years after Revere's death, so Revere might never have become famous. _____

8. Before that poem appeared, Paul Revere's name was not on any list of important people in America. _____

9. The increase in the number of times his name appeared on such lists after the poem was published was enough to make him famous. _____

10. Is fiction more powerful than fact? Is all our knowledge such a mixture of fact and fiction? _____

Van Goor and Hacker, *Developmental Exercises for The Bedford Handbook*, 9th ed. (Boston: Bedford, 2014)

11-3 | Mixed constructions 15

EXERCISE 11-4 ◆ Mixed constructions: Guided review

Edit the following paragraphs to eliminate problems with mixed constructions. The numbers in the margin refer to relevant rules in section 11 of *The Bedford Handbook*, Ninth Edition. The first revision has been done for you.

What did Paul Revere do when he wasn't working for the Revolution? Quite apart from his famous ride, Paul Revere made other significant contributions to American life and culture.

The basic reason for all these contributions was ~~because~~ *that* Paul Revere was an   11c
enterprising entrepreneur. He originally followed his father into silversmithing. Soon after the war started, he began making gunpowder. He designed and printed paper money and made the state seal that Massachusetts still uses. By carving false teeth   11a
from rhinoceros tusks was one of his efforts to make money; publishing hymnbooks was another. He engraved copperplates for printing. He ran a hardware store and erected barns for local farmers.

Until Revere built the first rolling mill for copper in the United States, so all   11a
rolled copper had to be imported. He set up the equipment to cast bronze and made cannon for the army, copper fittings for the USS *Constitution* (Old Ironsides), and bells for churches. Seventy-five of his bells still ring from New England church steeples.

As a silversmith, a very creative field, Revere displayed great skill. His silver   11b
pieces were so beautifully crafted that two hundred years later one of his punch bowls brought an offer of a hundred thousand dollars. One reason that antique lovers today search for silver objects marked "Revere" is because Revere's work is so graceful.   11c
Modern artisans still try to duplicate his decorated grooves and flowing lines. And shoppers admire certain smoothly curved bowls are known as Revere bowls whether   11a
they are made of silver or of some other metal.

Whether or not he rode all the way to Concord, Paul Revere made an indelible impression on American life and culture.

Van Goor and Hacker, *Developmental Exercises for The Bedford Handbook*, 9th ed. (Boston: Bedford, 2014)

EXERCISE 12-1 ◆ Misplaced and dangling modifiers: Guided practice

Edit the following paragraphs to eliminate misplaced and dangling modifiers. The numbers in the margin refer to relevant rules in section 12 of *The Bedford Handbook*, Ninth Edition. The first revision has been done for you; a suggested revision of this exercise appears in the back of this book.

people usually think first of
Hearing the name Karl Marx, Russia. is usually the first thought that comes to   12c

mind. Marx never lived in Russia at all. Actually, he almost spent all of his adult life   12a

in England. He was a political exile for the last half of his life.

Marx lived first in Germany. Born of Jewish parents, his university studies   12e

were completed with a PhD at the University of Jena. His favorite professor tried to

get Marx an appointment to teach at the university. When that professor was fired,

Marx gave up hope of teaching at Jena or any other German university. Marx, because   12c

he was denied a university position, had to earn his living as a journalist. He worked

briefly as a newspaper editor in Germany.

Next came France, Belgium, and a return to Germany. First Marx and his new

bride moved to Paris, where Marx worked for a radical journal and became friendly

with Friedrich Engels. When the journal ceased publication, Marx moved to Brussels,

Belgium, and then back to Cologne, Germany. He did not hold a regular job, so he tried

desperately to at least earn enough money to feed his family.   12d

Marx decided after living in Paris and Brussels he would settle in London. He   12b

and his family lived in abject poverty while Marx earned what little income he could

by writing for an American newspaper, the *New York Tribune*.

EXERCISE 12-2 ◆ Misplaced modifiers

To read about this topic, see section 12 in *The Bedford Handbook*, Ninth Edition.

Circle the letter of the more effective sentence in each pair. Example:

    a. **Marx almost spent all his time writing, using every waking moment to get his ideas down on paper.**

    (b.) **Marx spent almost all his time writing, using every waking moment to get his ideas down on paper.**

1. a. Between 1852 and 1862, Marx just wrote more than three hundred articles for the *New York Tribune*.

    b. Between 1852 and 1862, Marx wrote more than three hundred articles just for the *New York Tribune*.

2. a. During his lifetime, Marx did not receive much attention. But people all over the world paid attention to what he had written after his death.

    b. During his lifetime, Marx did not receive much attention. But after his death, people all over the world paid attention to what he had written.

3. a. He wanted only one thing for himself: recognition of the importance of his ideas.

    b. He only wanted one thing for himself: recognition of the importance of his ideas.

4. a. Capitalist scholars tend to usually say that Marx's work is "illogical" and "uninformed."

    b. Capitalist scholars usually tend to say that Marx's work is "illogical" and "uninformed."

5. a. However, most capitalists agree that as a student of social organization he was brilliant.

    b. However, most capitalists agree that he, as a student of social organization, was brilliant.

Van Goor and Hacker, *Developmental Exercises for The Bedford Handbook*, 9th ed. (Boston: Bedford, 2014)

EXERCISE 12-3 ◆ Misplaced and dangling modifiers

To read about this topic, see section 12 in *The Bedford Handbook*, Ninth Edition.

Circle the letter of the more effective sentence in each pair. Be prepared to explain your choice. Example:

  a. **Deciding that there were two classes of people in the world, they were named the "bourgeoisie" and the "proletariat."**

  (b.) **Deciding that there were two classes of people in the world, Marx named them the "bourgeoisie" and the "proletariat."**

1. a. Convinced that one major difference divided the people of the world into two groups, ownership of property was declared the basis for this division.

    b. Convinced that one major difference divided the people of the world into two groups, Marx declared that ownership of property was the basis for this division.

2. a. Marx defined anyone who owned property as bourgeois.

    b. Owning property of any kind, the property defined its owner as bourgeois.

3. a. Marx defined the proletariat as those who owned no property but labored to always produce wealth for the bourgeoisie.

    b. Marx defined the proletariat as those who owned no property but always labored to produce wealth for the bourgeoisie.

4. a. After finishing his study of economic history, Marx concluded that history is progressive and maybe even inevitable.

    b. Marx, after finishing his study of economic history, concluded that history is progressive and maybe even inevitable.

5. a. Denying God any role in human affairs, economic history was seen as a natural evolution in the world.

    b. Denying God any role in human affairs, Marx saw economic history as a natural evolution in the world.

Van Goor and Hacker, *Developmental Exercises for*
The Bedford Handbook, 9th ed. (Boston: Bedford, 2014)

12-3 | Misplaced and dangling modifiers **19**

EXERCISE 12-4 ◆ Misplaced and dangling modifiers: Guided review

Edit the following paragraphs to eliminate misplaced and dangling modifiers. The numbers in the margin refer to relevant rules in section 12 of *The Bedford Handbook*, Ninth Edition. The first revision has been done for you.

Marx wrote *The Communist Manifesto*, his most famous work, in collaboration with Friedrich Engels just before the German revolution of 1848. The book has three sections with distinct characteristics.

In the first section, Marx tries to ~~accurately~~ define terms *accurately* and to state his basic   12d
assumptions. He traces the class systems of earlier times and concludes that there are only two classes in his day, the bourgeoisie and the proletariat. The bourgeoisie are the property-owning capitalists; the proletariat are the working class. Marx asserts that as the bourgeoisie increase their economic power, they work toward their own eventual downfall.

Set up in question-and-answer format, Marx made the second section of his   12e
Communist Manifesto resemble a debate with a bourgeois sympathizer. Of course, Marx only sees one side of the debate as being correct. After "defeating" his opponent   12a
on major questions, Marx presents his own ten-point program in clear, easy-to-understand, persuasive language.

Marx, after developing the second section in detail, moves on to the *Manifesto*'s   12c
final section. He shows how Communists and other reform groups work toward the same goals. Reminding workers that they "have nothing to lose but their chains," Marx calls on them to zealously and actively work together. Marx utters the slogan that can   12d
still be heard today in ringing tones: "Workers of the world, unite!"   12b

Van Goor and Hacker, *Developmental Exercises for The Bedford Handbook*, 9th ed. (Boston: Bedford, 2014)

EXERCISE 13-1 ◆ Distracting shifts: Guided practice

Edit the following paragraphs to eliminate distracting shifts. The numbers in the margin refer to relevant rules in section 13 of *The Bedford Handbook*, Ninth Edition. The first revision has been done for you; a suggested revision of this exercise appears in the back of this book.

Do you know how slavery began in America or how ~~did it end~~? *it ended?* When the 13d
Mayflower landed in what is now Massachusetts in September 1620, slaves were
already in America. A Dutch ship had unloaded and sold twenty Africans in
Jamestown, Virginia, the year before.

Actually, slavery in America began long before that. Many early explorers
brought slaves with them to the new land, and some historians claim that one of the
men in Christopher Columbus's crew was a slave. From the 1500s to the 1800s, slave
ships brought ten million African slaves across the ocean.

Most of the slaves stayed in Latin America and the West Indies, but the
southern part of the United States received about 6 percent of them. Few northerners
owned slaves, and opposition to slavery was evident by the time of the American
Revolution. Rhode Island prohibited the importation of slaves even before the
Revolutionary War. After the war, six northern states abolish slavery at once, 13b
and other states pass laws to phase out slavery; even Virginia enacts legislation 13b
encouraging you to emancipate your slaves. 13a

But it took a war, a tricky political situation, and a very clever former slave
to free all slaves. History gives Abraham Lincoln the credit for liberating the slaves
during the Civil War, and he deserves some credit, but emancipation was not his idea.
Originally, no one in government seriously considered emancipation because they were 13a
so focused on winning the war to save the Union. Then an important black man talks 13b
to Lincoln and gives him the idea and the reason. This man said that freeing slaves
would be good for the war effort and would Lincoln agree to do it? Who was this man? 13d
He was Frederick Douglass, fugitive slave and newspaper editor.

EXERCISE 13-2 ◆ Distracting shifts

To read about this topic, see section 13 in *The Bedford Handbook*, Ninth Edition.

A Edit the following sentences to eliminate distracting pronoun shifts. If a sentence is correct, mark it "OK." Example:

Frederick Douglass was born a slave, but he was lucky because his owner's wife did not

know that it was against the law for ~~you~~ to teach a slave to read and write.
her

1. A slave who learned to read and write gained self-confidence, so they were harder to oversee than illiterate slaves.

2. When he had learned enough to study on his own own, the slave Frederick Douglass did so; he used what he had learned to escape from his owner.

3. The master had told his slaves that all escape routes were blocked and that you would have no chance whatever at success.

4. Douglass used a simple but dangerous method of escape; he sailed from Baltimore to New York as a working sailor.

5. A listener could not learn anything about escape routes from Douglass's stories because Douglass told them nothing that would endanger other fugitives.

B Edit the following sentences to eliminate distracting shifts in verb tense. If a sentence is correct, mark it "OK." Example:

Douglass's narrative tells about his own life as a child and ~~described~~ his torturous beatings
describes

by a professional "slave breaker."

6. Douglass had few ties to his mother and never meets his father.

7. Even when Douglass worked "out" for his master, his master got his wages.

8. His master sometimes allowed him to keep 1 percent (six cents out of six dollars); the master thought the money would encourage Douglass to work harder.

9. Douglass escapes by pretending to be someone else; he borrowed the identification papers of a freed black sailor.

10. Frederick Douglass used several different last names as he escaped slavery; an abolitionist friend suggests the name Douglass to him, and Frederick uses it from that time on.

Van Goor and Hacker, *Developmental Exercises for The Bedford Handbook*, 9th ed. (Boston: Bedford, 2014)

EXERCISE 13-3 ◆ Distracting shifts

To read about this topic, see section 13 in *The Bedford Handbook*, Ninth Edition.

Edit the following sentences to eliminate shifts between direct and indirect quotations or questions. Example:

whether he
When Frederick was told to choose a new name, he asked could he keep Frederick and
^

take a new last name.

1. When a friend suggested Douglass as a last name, Frederick asked whether it was a satisfactory name and did it fit well with Frederick?

2. People frequently asked Douglass how did he feel when he found himself in a free state.

3. Lonely and frightened at the time, he said, "I can trust no man" and that he saw every white man as an enemy, every black man as a cause for distrust.

4. Douglass was befriended by David Ruggles, an abolitionist who asked him what did he plan to do.

5. Douglass married Anna and told her that they would move to New Bedford and don't worry because he would surely get a job there.

Van Goor and Hacker, *Developmental Exercises for*
The Bedford Handbook, 9th ed. (Boston: Bedford, 2014)

13-3 | Distracting shifts   **23**

EXERCISE 13-4 ◆ Distracting shifts: Guided review

Edit the following paragraphs to eliminate any distracting shifts. The numbers in the margin refer to relevant rules in section 13 of *The Bedford Handbook*, Ninth Edition. The first revision has been done for you.

Frederick Douglass, who was born a slave and became a much-sought-after lecturer and writer, was a man of strong will and convictions.

Douglass never hesitated to defend the choices he ~~makes~~ *made* for himself and his   13b
family. On trains he sat in cars reserved for "whites only" until security officers
dragged him away. He walked out of a church when it was realized that none of his   13c
people could participate in the service until the white people were finished.

Wherever he lived, Douglass fought slavery. When he published his autobiography, *Narrative of the Life of Frederick Douglass*, in 1845, he was still a fugitive
slave. He and his wife moved to England the same year because he feared that his
book would reveal his identity as a fugitive slave. Also, some of his other writings had
aroused so much animosity that he fears for his life. From England, he wrote letters   13b
and worked to gain support for freeing the slaves. After friends in England raised
enough money to buy his freedom for him, he was even more determined to help
others gain their freedom. (Slaves used to say that a free black was never there when
you needed help, but no one could ever say that about Frederick Douglass.)   13a

Douglass was outspoken in his support for the causes he believed in. When the
Civil War broke out, Douglass comes back to the United States to help recruit African   13b
Americans to fight. "This war is for you and your children," he told them. Douglass
also supported woman suffrage, and he defended the right of members of different
races to marry if they wished. When Douglass married his second wife, a white
woman, critics complained. He answered them by saying, "My first wife was the color
of my mother" and that the second was the color of his father, so he was not playing   13d
favorites.

Van Goor and Hacker, *Developmental Exercises for
The Bedford Handbook*, 9th ed. (Boston: Bedford, 2014)

EXERCISE 14-1 ◆ Emphasis: Guided practice

Edit the following paragraph to put major ideas in independent clauses and minor ideas in subordinate clauses or phrases. The numbers in the margin refer to relevant rules in section 14 of *The Bedford Handbook*, Ninth Edition. The first revision has been done for you; a suggested revision of this exercise appears in the back of this book.

No one who knew Albert Einstein as a young child would ever have believed that he might one day be called the smartest man in the world. None of his teachers could have predicted success for him. ~~Albert was a~~ A shy, slow learner. ~~He was shy. He~~ Albert   **14b**
always got into trouble in class. He consistently failed some subjects. They were the   **14b**
subjects he did not like. His family could not have predicted his success either. Albert could not even get to meals on time. Night after night his parents had to postpone dinner until servants searched the house and grounds and found the boy, at which   **14e**
time he would be full of apologies but have no explanation to offer for his lateness except that he was "thinking." Once his angry father dangled his big gold watch at Albert. He told Albert to figure out how late he was. Albert, who was fascinated by   **14b, 14d**
the tiny magnetic compass hanging from the watch chain, could not tell time. The boy asked so many questions about the compass that he did not eat much dinner anyway. Albert begged his father to lend him the compass to sleep with, and his father let him   **14c**
borrow it. Years later Einstein wondered whether that little compass had been the beginning of his interest in science.

Van Goor and Hacker, *Developmental Exercises for*
The Bedford Handbook, 9th ed. (Boston: Bedford, 2014)

14-1 | Emphasis: Guided practice   **25**

EXERCISE 14-2 ◆ Emphasis

To read about this topic, see section 14 in *The Bedford Handbook*, Ninth Edition.

Combine or restructure the following sentences so that the independent clause expresses the idea in brackets and everything else is subordinated. Example:

> *who owned an electrochemical factory,*
> **Albert Einstein's father, Hermann Einstein, had some interest in science. ~~He owned an~~**
> ^
> **~~electrochemical factory.~~ [Emphasize his father's interest in science.]**

1. Hermann Einstein moved his electrochemical business to Munich; the move made it possible for his son to have the best schooling available. [Emphasize the fact that Hermann moved his business.]

2. Albert Einstein's Uncle Jake explained math to the boy and made algebra problems into games. [Emphasize Uncle Jake's making games out of the problems.]

3. Albert's mother was impressed by her son's persistent questions and secretly hoped that Albert would one day be a professor. [Emphasize the mother's hope.]

4. One of Albert's friends was a medical student at the University of Munich. This friend supplied Albert with well-written modern books on natural science. [Emphasize that the friend supplied Einstein with books.]

5. Hermann Einstein kept his business in Munich for several years, and afterward he decided to go to Italy and work with relatives. [Emphasize the decision to go to Italy and work with relatives.]

Van Goor and Hacker, *Developmental Exercises for The Bedford Handbook*, 9th ed. (Boston: Bedford, 2014)

EXERCISE 14-3 ◆ Emphasis

To read about this topic, see section 14 in *The Bedford Handbook*, Ninth Edition.

Combine or restructure the following sentences so that the independent clause expresses the idea mentioned in brackets. Example:

> *When*
> **Hermann Einstein moved his family to Italy, ~~but~~ he left Albert in Munich to finish school.**
> ^
> **[Emphasize his leaving Albert in Munich to finish school.]**

1. Albert was miserably lonely without his family, and he had always depended on them for his social life. [Emphasize Albert's loneliness without his family.]

2. He did not get along with the other students. He did not get along with his teachers either. [Emphasize both ideas equally.]

3. He had never gotten along well with other students, and they envied his superior work in math and physics. [Emphasize his not getting along with other students.]

4. In mathematics he was smarter than his teachers, so his teachers resented him too. [Emphasize his teachers' resentment of him.]

5. He was desperate to be with his family in sunny Italy, so he faked a nervous breakdown. [Emphasize his faking a nervous breakdown.]

6. Albert convinced a medical doctor to sign a formal request for a six-month vacation, and then he found out that the school had expelled him. [Emphasize his discovery that the school had expelled him.]

7. His months in Italy were a welcome change, and they gave him time to enjoy life again and to plan for his future. [Emphasize that the months in Italy were a welcome change.]

8. Albert spent months thinking about his future while he enjoyed Italy's scenery, art, and music, and then he finally decided that he wanted to be a theoretical physicist. [Emphasize his decision to become a theoretical physicist.]

9. He knew that his father's business was not doing well, but he asked his father for enough money to take the entrance exams at the Swiss Federal Polytechnic School. [Emphasize his request to his father.]

10. His father wanted Albert to succeed, so he found the money somehow. [Emphasize his father's finding the money.]

Van Goor and Hacker, *Developmental Exercises for*
The Bedford Handbook, 9th ed. (Boston: Bedford, 2014)

14-3 | Emphasis **27**

EXERCISE 14-4 ◆ Emphasis: Guided review

Edit the following paragraph to put major ideas in independent clauses and minor ideas in subordinate clauses or phrases. The numbers in the margin refer to relevant rules in section 14 of *The Bedford Handbook*, Ninth Edition. The first revision has been done for you.

Teachers are not always right about their pupils. Certainly Albert Einstein's

misjudging

teachers, ~~misjudged~~ his ability in math, ~~and they~~ failed to spot the most brilliant   14c

student they had ever had. Giuseppe Verdi's teachers made similar errors in judging

their pupil's musical ability. Verdi was Italian. He lived in the nineteenth century.   14b

He wanted to be a composer. He applied to the Conservatory of Music in Milan, and   14c

he was rejected because he "showed no aptitude for music." Today his works are

performed more than those of any other opera composer. Scientists have also been

underestimated. Everyone has heard of Charles Darwin, the British scientist. This

man, who also had trouble in school, was the first to propose the theory of evolution.   14d

He did so poorly at his school, which was the University of Edinburgh, that his   14e

teachers considered him hopeless, as a result of which they dismissed him. The first

American physicist to win the Nobel Prize for physics was also misjudged by his

teachers. Albert Abraham Michelson was a student at Annapolis. He was in the naval   14b

academy there. One of his teachers told him to pay less attention to science and

concentrate on naval gunnery. Luckily, Einstein, Verdi, Darwin, and Michelson refused

to accept their teachers' evaluations of them.

Van Goor and Hacker, *Developmental Exercises for The Bedford Handbook*, 9th ed. (Boston: Bedford, 2014)

EXERCISE 15-1 ◆ Variety: Guided practice

The following paragraphs are grammatically correct but dull. Revise them to add variety. You may need to combine some sentences. The numbers in the margin refer to relevant revision strategies in section 15 of *The Bedford Handbook*, Ninth Edition. The first revision has been done for you; a suggested revision of this exercise appears in the back of this book.

After studying

Everyone has heard of Martin Luther King Jr. ~~He studied~~ for the ministry at

                                            15b, 15a
                                            (See also
                                               15c.)

earning

Boston University and ~~earned~~ a doctorate in theology, ~~and then~~ he went home to the

South to work as a minister. He started working in civil rights and became the

most influential leader of that cause in America. When he died, the victim of an

assassin's bullet, his name was almost synonymous with "civil rights." Historians and

biographers have recorded his leadership in the fight to gain basic civil rights for all

Americans. Many people who know of his civil rights work, however, are not aware of

his skill as a writer. King produced other important writing in addition to his carefully   15b

crafted and emotional speeches.

King's "Letter from Birmingham Jail" is among his most famous writings. He   15c

wrote it to answer a statement published by eight Alabama ministers that King's   15b, 15a
                                                                                        (See also
work was "unwise and untimely," and the letter shows King to be a man who had great   15c.)

patience with his critics. King is eager to get these ministers to accept his point of   15a
                                                                                        (See also
view, so he reminds them that they are ministers. Their goodwill, he says, should help   15c.)

them see that his views hold value. He does not attack them personally. He analyzes   15a
                                                                                        (See also
their arguments. Then he presents his own views. Does he use many of the emotional   14b.)

appeals for which he is justly famous? No, in this letter King depends on logic and

reasoning as the tools to win his argument.

EXERCISE 15-2 ◆ Variety

To read about this topic, see section 15 in *The Bedford Handbook*, Ninth Edition.

Edit each of the following sentences in at least two ways, to provide varied openings and varied sentence structures. You may need to change other parts of each sentence as well. Example:

                                               In   *Martin Luther King Jr.*

   a.   ~~Martin Luther King Jr. was in~~ jail awaiting a hearing**/,** ~~he~~ read a newspaper article

       attacking his work.

       When

   b.   Martin Luther King Jr. was in jail awaiting a hearing**/,** he read a newspaper article

       attacking his work.

1. a. King didn't have much to write on in the jail, so he started writing in the margins of the newspaper in which the article appeared.

   b. King didn't have much to write on in the jail, so he started writing in the margins of the newspaper in which the article appeared.

2. a. A black trusty, wanting to help King, was able to get some scraps of paper for him after a while.

   b. A black trusty, wanting to help King, was able to get some scraps of paper for him after a while.

3. a. His attorneys were later allowed to give him a pad of paper. King, fired up by the newspaper article, quickly filled the pad.

   b. His attorneys were later allowed to give him a pad of paper. King, fired up by the newspaper article, quickly filled the pad.

4. a. King chose to write his response to the newspaper article in letter form, so he seemed like the biblical Paul to some people.

   b. King chose to write his response to the newspaper article in letter form, so he seemed like the biblical Paul to some people.

5. a. How were King and Paul alike? Paul, a preacher of the Christian faith like King, wrote some of his famous letters from a prison cell.

   b. How were King and Paul alike? Paul, a preacher of the Christian faith like King, wrote some of his famous letters from a prison cell.

Van Goor and Hacker, *Developmental Exercises for The Bedford Handbook*, 9th ed. (Boston: Bedford, 2014)

EXERCISE 15-3 ◆ Variety: Guided review

The following paragraph is grammatically correct but dull. Revise it to add variety. You may need to combine some sentences. The numbers in the margin refer to relevant revision strategies in section 15 of *The Bedford Handbook*, Ninth Edition. The first revision has been done for you.

Martin Luther King Jr.'s famous "Letter from Birmingham Jail" has a clearly
thought-out structure. ~~King begins~~ *Beginning* with the statement that any nonviolent campaign
has to go through four distinct stages. /~~He says these stages are~~ fact finding,   15a or 15b
negotiation, self-purification, and direct action./~~He~~ *--King* says that he and his fellow
campaigners have gone through all these steps in Birmingham. King tries to reach his
readers after that beginning by asking them how to answer his children's questions   15a
about why they cannot go to the amusement park advertised on TV. The letter
discusses the difference between just and unjust laws, and it emphasizes the need for   15a or 15b
nonviolent direct action to dramatize the unjust ones. Next King mentions the "white   (See also
moderates." He expresses his disappointment with white churches and white religious   15c.)
leaders who have failed to join the civil rights movement, but he praises the few who
have helped. He describes the mistreatment he and his friends have suffered at the   15a or 15b
hands of the local police, and he gives thanks for the courage of the people involved in   (See also
sit-ins and bus strikes. King writes finally of his faith that the movement will survive   15c.)
and prosper and that racial prejudice will soon pass away.   15b

Van Goor and Hacker, *Developmental Exercises for
The Bedford Handbook*, 9th ed. (Boston: Bedford, 2014)

15-3 | Variety: Guided review   **31**

REVIEW OF 8–15 ◆ Clear sentences

Edit the following paragraphs to eliminate sentence problems. Section numbers in the margin refer to suggested revision strategies in *The Bedford Handbook*, Ninth Edition. The first revision has been done for you.

One of the men who greatly influenced Martin Luther King Jr. was Mahatma

Gandhi, ~~and he~~ *who* introduced nonviolent protest techniques in Africa and India. Gandhi   14c

is called the father of his country, and he helped India gain its freedom from England.   14c

Gandhi's nonviolent method was based on three principles: courage, being truthful,

and you had to have endurance. By using nonviolent techniques is how Gandhi helped   9a, 11a

Indians in Africa and India.

After studying law in London, he attempts to practice law in India but is   13b

not very successful. When he went to South Africa to do legal work in 1893, he was

abused because he was an Indian who also claimed the rights of a British subject.

Although he had planned to stay in Africa one year, he remained for twenty-one years.

Fighting injustice in South Africa, the principle of *satyagraha* (nonviolent protest) was   12e

developed by Gandhi during those years.   8a

After working in South Africa, Gandhi returned to India to lead the Indian

movement for independence. While in India, he led hundreds of his followers on a

march to the sea. There they made salt from seawater to protest a law. That law   14b

required them to buy all their salt from the government. He also began programs of

hand weaving and spinning among the poor that exist to this day.   12b

Although Gandhi believed and lived by the nonviolent principle of *satyagraha*,   10a

he died a violent death. In 1948, he was assassinated by a high-caste Hindu fanatic.

This man feared Gandhi's tolerance for all creeds and religions. Nevertheless,   14b

Gandhi's nonviolent methods have survived to this day. When Martin Luther King

Jr. began his civil rights work in the United States, many people compared him to

Gandhi, saying that his principles were essentially the same as Gandhi.   10c

Van Goor and Hacker, *Developmental Exercises for The Bedford Handbook*, 9th ed. (Boston: Bedford, 2014)

EXERCISE 16-1 ◆ Wordy sentences: Guided practice

Edit the following paragraphs to make any wordy sentences as short as possible without changing their meaning. The numbers in the margin refer to relevant rules in section 16 of *The Bedford Handbook*, Ninth Edition. The first two revisions have been done for you; a suggested revision of this exercise appears in the back of this book.

The establishment of the National Park Service was set in motion in 1912 when forty-five-year-old Stephen Mather was ~~engaged in~~ hiking in California's Sequoia   16d

National Park and met ~~a person by the name of~~ John Muir, the famous wilderness   16c

advocate who had founded the Sierra Club. Two years after that influential visit,

Mather visited Sequoia and Yosemite and was appalled due to the fact that the parks   16c

were not being maintained in a proper manner. When he complained in a letter of   16b

complaint to Franklin Lane, who held the position of secretary of the interior in   16a

Washington, DC, Lane wrote back: "Dear Steve, If you don't like the way the parks are

being run, come on down to Washington and run them yourself."

Stephen Mather reacted and responded by going to Washington, DC, and   16b

becoming Lane's assistant. In 1916, the National Park Service was established, and

Mather became its first director. He believed so strongly in the establishment and

preservation of national parks that he paid the salaries of employees who worked for   16a

him from his own pocket. In addition, he convinced benefactors to purchase land for   16c

the purpose of donating it for national parks. He even purchased land on his own and

donated it to the National Park Service.

In addition to being a longtime member of the Sierra Club, Stephen Mather

had another, more personal motivation to preserve wilderness areas for future

generations. Mather suffered from severe bouts of depression, so he often sought out

the wilderness, which was a place that provided solace for him.   16e

Following Mather's death on January 22, 1930, many national parks honored

him by displaying a plaque with words that stated: "There will never come an end to   16a

the good that he has done."

Van Goor and Hacker, *Developmental Exercises for*
The Bedford Handbook, 9th ed. (Boston: Bedford, 2014)

16-1 | Wordy sentences: Guided practice   **33**

EXERCISE 16-2 ◆ Wordy sentences

To read about this topic, see section 16 in *The Bedford Handbook*, Ninth Edition.

Tighten the following sentences by eliminating redundancies, unnecessary repetition, and empty phrases. The number in parentheses at the end of each sentence is a suggested maximum number of words for your revised sentence. Example:

> **The National Park Service expanded and improved in ~~the time period of~~ the early 1930s**
>
> **following the end of ~~the era known as~~ the Great Depression. (18)**

1. Franklin D. Roosevelt played a significant role in the growth and expansion of the National Park Service when he was responsible for the creation of the Civilian Conservation Corps. (22)

2. The Civilian Conservation Corps was a work relief program whose objective and goal at that point in time was to develop and maintain government-owned land such as state and national parks. (24. A hyphenated word counts as one word.)

3. This program, which was established in the year of 1933, was part of President Roosevelt's "New Deal" to restore America's economy in order to put people back to work. (22)

4. Through the CCC, there were new state parks that were developed, and national parks were upgraded with upgrades such as better roads, facilities, and trails. (19)

5. By 1942, when the CCC program came to an end, around the number of nine hundred state, county, and city parks had been created, and ninety-four national parks and monuments had been improved. (27. A hyphenated word counts as one word.)

Van Goor and Hacker, *Developmental Exercises for The Bedford Handbook*, 9th ed. (Boston: Bedford, 2014)

EXERCISE 16-3 ◆ Wordy sentences

To read about this topic, see section 16 in *The Bedford Handbook*, Ninth Edition.

Tighten the following sentences without changing their meaning. The number in parentheses at the end of each sentence is a suggested maximum number of words for your revised sentence. Example:

> In addition to providing various ~~and different~~ recreational opportunities for families, the
> National Park Service strives to preserve America's history ~~in terms of culture.~~ (19)
> *cultural* (inserted above "history")

1. The National Park Service is an agency that manages hundreds of historic parks, landmarks, and monuments for the purpose of commemoration, appreciation, and education. (17)

2. One historical site is the Johnson House, located in the city of Philadelphia. In the 1850s, the Johnson family provided a safe haven for fugitive slaves who were in the process of using the Underground Railroad to seek their freedom. (30)

3. On the remote and out-of-the-way location of Seward Peninsula in Alaska is the Bering Land Bridge National Preserve, which protects what remains of a natural land bridge that connected Asia with North America during a period more than 13,000 years ago. (34)

4. The Bering Land Bridge National Preserve can be accessed by visitors only by bush plane or boat in the summer and by means of ski plane, snowmobile, or even dogsled in the winter. (30)

5. The Martin Luther King Jr. National Historic Site in Atlanta, Georgia, features the birth home of civil rights leader Martin Luther King Jr.; Ebenezer Baptist Church, the church where he preached; and the site of his grave. (32)

6. The National Park Service is also the agency that manages the Trail of Tears National Historic Trail, a two-thousand-mile route that commemorates the Cherokee walk from the southern Appalachians to the state of Oklahoma, an event that cost thousands of Cherokees their lives. (36)

7. In southern Arizona, the Tumacácori National Historical Park is a park that preserves three Spanish mission ruins dating from the period of time of the late seventeenth and eighteenth centuries. (21)

8. The National Park Service also preserves and protects historic battlefields, for example, the Big Hole National Battlefield, which is located in the area of southwest Montana. (18)

Van Goor and Hacker, *Developmental Exercises for
The Bedford Handbook*, 9th ed. (Boston: Bedford, 2014)

16-3 | Wordy sentences   35

9. The Big Hole National Battlefield commemorates the Battle of Big Hole, which is a battle that was fought between the Nez Perce and the US government in the month of August in 1877. (23)

10. The National Park Service provides recreational and educational opportunities for all people in America and around the world. At the present time, it manages more than eighty-four million acres of national parks, monuments, landmarks, recreation areas, and historic sites, including the White House. (37)

Van Goor and Hacker, *Developmental Exercises for*
The Bedford Handbook, 9th ed. (Boston: Bedford, 2014)

EXERCISE 16-4 ◆ Wordy sentences: Guided review

Edit the following paragraph to make any wordy sentences as short as possible without changing their meaning. The numbers in the margin refer to relevant rules in section 16 of *The Bedford Handbook*, Ninth Edition. The first wordy sentence has been revised for you.

As the National Park Service anticipates its centennial anniversary in ~~the year~~   16a

~~of~~ 2016, the secretary of the interior has outlined some specific goals for ~~the purpose~~   16c

~~of~~ continuing the conservation, preservation, and enjoyment of national parks,

monuments, and historic sites. There is an important goal that involves rehabilitating   16d

buildings that are historic in nature, restoring native habitats, and improving natural   16d

resources. Another goal calls for environmental leadership, which involves the act of   16c

demonstrating better environmental practices and using alternative energy and fuel

sources. The National Park Service also plans and intends to use more volunteers who   16b

can work without pay to help maintain trails and improve recreational experiences for   16b

visitors who come to the park. Finally, it is the intention of the National Park Service   16b, 16c

to improve educational experiences in national parks and monuments by expanding

the junior ranger program and creating richer interactive Web sites.

EXERCISE 17-1 ◆ Appropriate language: Guided practice

A The writer of the following paragraph used language that is too informal for the audience—an educated group of nonexperts. Revise the paragraph by replacing slang, regional expressions, nonstandard English, and sexist language. The numbers in the margin refer to relevant rules in section 17 of
The Bedford Handbook, Ninth Edition. The first revision has been done for you; a suggested revision
of this exercise appears in the back of this book.

most impressive

One of America's ~~coolest~~ national parks is Grand Canyon National Park in   17d
      ^

northern Arizona. Established as a national park in 1919, it is now one of America's

hottest landmarks. Each year, nearly five million visitors come to the park to feast   17d, 17d

their eyes on this spectacular and colorful canyon. Ask a park ranger, and he will tell   17f

you that the canyon is nearly a mile deep in places and between ten and eighteen

miles wide. The canyon was formed over several million years by the flow of the

Colorado River. Although it ain't the world's deepest canyon, it is one of the most   17d

ginormous examples of the power of erosion.   17d

B The writer of the following paragraph used too much puffed-up language for an audience of educated nonexperts. Revise the paragraph, replacing jargon, pretentious language, and sexist language.
Numbers in the margin refer to relevant rules in section 17 of *The Bedford Handbook*, Ninth Edition.
The first revision has been done for you; a suggested revision of this exercise appears in the back
of this book.

Recreational activities

~~Activities related to the pursuit of recreation~~ are numerous in Grand Canyon   17b
                                            ^

National Park. A round-trip hike to the bottom of the canyon is a memorable

experience, but the steep, rugged trails can be a challenge, even for hikers who have   17b

previously engaged in hiking experiences. Hikers must carry their own water and

be prepared for extreme temperatures. Those who prefer not to hike can ride a mule

down into the canyon or ambulate along the easy and level trails along the rim.   17b

Park rangers offer guided walking tours and will make available by means of oral   17b

communication information about the park's history, culture, and geology. Just a mile

from the Market Plaza is the Yavapai Geology Museum, which displays photographs

and exhibits explaining the park's geological history. Whatever the visitor's dwell time   17a

at park attractions, she can count on breathtaking views.   17f

Van Goor and Hacker, *Developmental Exercises for*
The Bedford Handbook, 9th ed. (Boston: Bedford, 2014)

EXERCISE 17-2 ◆ Appropriate language

To read about this topic, see section 17 in *The Bedford Handbook*, Ninth Edition.

Change the italicized words and phrases in the following sentences to more appropriate language for an educated audience of nonexperts. Consult the dictionary if necessary. Do not change the meaning of any sentence. Example:

> The history and culture of Grand Canyon National Park are enriched by two Native
> American tribes who ~~make their domiciles~~ *live* on the South Rim of the canyon.

1. Centuries ago, the Havasupai, which means "people of the blue-green waters," lived in the canyon during the spring and summer and *conveyed their movable assets* to the South Rim during the fall and winter.

2. Today, the Havasupai people live in Havasu Canyon and welcome visitors to their reservation to *participate in attaining data* about their culture and authentic art and jewelry.

3. On the Havasupai reservation are four spring-fed waterfalls where visitors can *chill* in the turquoise-colored pools.

4. The ten-mile trail to the pools is accessible only by foot or by *equestrian*; however, visitors must plan to *crash* in a campground or in the Havasupai Lodge to take advantage of the beautiful falls and pools.

5. After visiting Havasu Falls, one visitor *articulated in writing* the following: "Imagine for a moment turquoise melting in your hand, its vibrant blue becoming liquid, and you will have in mind the stunning beauty waiting for you at Havasu Falls."

6. The "People of the Tall Pines," the Hualapai Tribe, have more *affiliates and familial groups* than the Havasupai Tribe and live on a reservation of nearly one million acres along the South Rim of the Grand Canyon and the Colorado River.

7. Most of the Hualapai tribe members live in Peach Springs, about fifty-five miles east of Kingman, Arizona, where their *pecuniary resources* depend heavily on cattle and tourism.

8. The Hualapai Tribe constructed the famous Skywalk, *an orbicular-shaped* platform that extends seventy feet over the edge of the Grand Canyon.

Van Goor and Hacker, *Developmental Exercises for The Bedford Handbook*, 9th ed. (Boston: Bedford, 2014)

17-2 | Appropriate language   **39**

9. The Skywalk is made of solid glass, so visitors can walk out over the edge of *this big hole in the ground* and see the canyon floor far below their feet.

10. These two tribes have *assimilated their habituated daily activities and customs* with the public yet have maintained their rich culture and heritage.

Van Goor and Hacker, *Developmental Exercises for The Bedford Handbook,* 9th ed. (Boston: Bedford, 2014)

EXERCISE 17-3 ◆ Appropriate language

To read about this topic, see section 17 in *The Bedford Handbook*, Ninth Edition.

Circle the letter of the more appropriately worded sentence in each pair. Assume an educated audience of nonexperts, and be prepared to explain your choices. Example:

(**a.**) **Grand Canyon National Park has an alliance with the Museum of Northern Arizona to preserve artifacts uncovered by natural erosion along the Colorado River.**

b. **Grand Canyon National Park has an alliance with the Museum of Northern Arizona to preserve artifacts uncovered by the progressive superficial loss of sediment along the Colorado River.**

1. a. Since the National Park Service maintains a "preservation-in-place" policy, excavations are limited to extraneous and artificial articles that cannot be preserved unless moved.

   b. Since the National Park Service maintains a "preservation-in-place" policy, excavations are limited to artifacts that cannot be preserved unless moved.

2. a. After excavation work began in 2007, archaeologists were excited to unearth three Pueblo masonry rooms in an area called Furnace Flats.

   b. After excavation work began in 2007, archaeologists were stoked to unearth three Pueblo masonry rooms in an area called Furnace Flats.

3. a. At Furnace Flats, archaeologists brought to light through exploration ceramic gaming pieces, stone pendants, and tools used for grinding food.

   b. At Furnace Flats, archaeologists discovered ceramic gaming pieces, stone pendants, and tools used for grinding food.

4. a. One of the most exciting finds was a kiva, an underground circular room that was most likely used in ceremonial rituals.

   b. One of the most exciting finds was a kiva, a subterranean circular room that was most likely used in prescribed ceremonial-related procedures.

5. a. These artifacts, which are on display at the Grand Canyon Park Museum, provide awesome insights into the lives of ancient people who lived in the canyon along the Colorado River.

   b. These artifacts, which are on display at the Grand Canyon Park Museum, provide valuable insight into the lives of ancient people who lived in the canyon along the Colorado River.

Van Goor and Hacker, *Developmental Exercises for The Bedford Handbook*, 9th ed. (Boston: Bedford, 2014)

17-3 | Appropriate language   **41**

EXERCISE 17-4 ◆ Appropriate language: Guided review

Revise the following paragraph using Standard English free of slang, jargon, pretentious language, and sexist language. The numbers in the margin refer to relevant rules in section 17 of *The Bedford Handbook*, Ninth Edition. The first sentence has been revised for you.

When the Grand Canyon is mentioned, most people ~~ruminate~~ *think* only about the | 17b

more popular South Rim. The North Rim of the Grand Canyon, however, is also part

of the national park and offers what many claim are equally spectacular views. The

North Rim is simply more in the boondocks. Lying at the edge of the Kaibab Plateau, | 17d

the North Rim can be reached via scenic Highway 67, a 210-mile drive from the

South Rim. If a tourist wants to hike to the North Rim, he can expect an arduous | 17f

21-mile hike that will take two to three days. Visitors will find a few uncool things on | 17d

the north side of the canyon. Because of its high elevation, over 8,000 feet, Highway

67 is generally barred to vehicular traffic from mid-October through mid-May. Also, | 17b

visitors with respiratory problems may find the air uncomfortably thin. Finally, cell

phone service may be limited. Nevertheless, the North Rim appeals to those who

prefer a place to chill. Several hiking trails are available as well as mule rides along | 17d

the rim or down into the canyon. The bucolic Grand Canyon Lodge at the North Rim | 17b

is a National Historic Landmark, with a restaurant featuring menu items that are | 17b

produced without the use of chemically formulated fertilizers. Many visitors take

advantage of the North Rim's location and include visits to Zion National Park, Bryce

Canyon, Lake Powell, or even Las Vegas. While the North Rim will never be as popular

as the South Rim, it will always be a rewarding and memorable experience.

Van Goor and Hacker, *Developmental Exercises for The Bedford Handbook*, 9th ed. (Boston: Bedford, 2014)

EXERCISE 18-1 ◆ Exact words: Guided practice

In the following paragraph, replace general words with specific ones and revise clichés and mixed figures of speech. Be sure that connotations are appropriate, that idioms are used properly, and that words are not misused. The numbers in the margin refer to relevant rules in section 18 of *The Bedford Handbook*, Ninth Edition. The first revision has been done for you; a suggested revision of this exercise appears in the back of this book.

Thousands of years before Yosemite Valley became one of America's ~~trendiest~~ *most popular* 18a

national parks, the Miwok and Paiute tribes lived there. They categorized themselves 18c

the Ahwahneechee, after their name for the valley, "Ahwahnee," which means "place

of the gaping mouth." In 1851, the Ahwahneechee were convicted from the valley 18c

after conflicts with miners during the Gold Rush era. Later, in 1889, the famous

naturalist John Muir persuaded Congress to protect the valley's high country from the

annihilation caused by grazing sheep. Thus, in 1890, more than 1,500 square miles 18a

became Yosemite National Park, currently one of America's most infamous vacation 18c

destinations. Most people are familiar about El Capitan, an iconic Yosemite Valley 18d

landmark, a nearly vertical granite rock formation that rises about 3,000 feet from

the valley floor to its summit. Another widely recognized thing is Half Dome, whose 18b

western face forms a sheer granite wall. Waterfalls, sequoia trees, and clear mountain

streams abound as far as the eye can see, drawing more than 3.5 million visitors 18e

annually to this crown jewel of the National Park Service.

Van Goor and Hacker, *Developmental Exercises for The Bedford Handbook*, 9th ed. (Boston: Bedford, 2014)

18-1 | Exact words: Guided practice **43**

EXERCISE 18-2 ◆ Exact words

To read about this topic, see section 18 in *The Bedford Handbook*, Ninth Edition.

A In each of the following sentences, circle the more specific word or phrase in parentheses. Example:

John Muir was a famous (person / (naturalist)) who founded the Sierra Club and whose writing encouraged the preservation and conservation of wilderness areas.

1. One wilderness area that John Muir especially loved is (America's / California's) Yosemite National Park.

2. While John Muir lived in Yosemite from 1868 through 1874, his love for the (Sierra Nevada / mountains) grew strong.

3. He wrote in (a publication / the Sierra Club bulletin), "Climb the mountains and get their good tidings. Nature's peace will flow into you as sunshine into trees."

4. In the late 1880s, Muir grew increasingly concerned about the damage grazing (sheep / livestock) were doing to the land.

5. In an article published in *Century Magazine*, Muir contended that (Yosemite / the land) could be saved from further damage if it were designated a national park.

B Edit the following sentences to replace words with inappropriate connotations. (See a thesaurus, the glossary of usage [p. 818] in *The Bedford Handbook*, Ninth Edition, or a dictionary if necessary.) Example:

          persuasive
John Muir's ~~argumentative~~ magazine article about the need to protect Yosemite helped convince Congress to propose a bill to create Yosemite National Park.

6. Thanks to Muir's labor, Yosemite became a national park in 1890.

7. Muir continued to write about the need to defend wilderness areas, not just for their beauty but also for ecological conservation.

8. His poetic writings stimulated travelers from around the world to come to the Sierra Nevada as well as to other wilderness areas in America.

9. Muir's writing also played a drastic role in the designation of Grand Canyon and Sequoia as national parks.

10. While John Muir prized all of nature, his favorite place was probably the Sierra Nevada, where he spent many happy hours hiking and enjoying their beauty.

Van Goor and Hacker, *Developmental Exercises for The Bedford Handbook*, 9th ed. (Boston: Bedford, 2014)

EXERCISE 18-3 ◆ Exact words

To read about this topic, see section 18 in *The Bedford Handbook*, Ninth Edition.

A Circle the correct word or expression in parentheses. Example:

Yosemite National Park's Half Dome (⟨rises⟩/ raises) to a height of 8,800 feet above (see /⟨sea⟩) level.

1. (Its / It's) majestic beauty attracts countless hikers (who's / whose) goal is to reach Half Dome's summit.

2. Visitors are so (enthusiastic / enthused) about hiking Half Dome that the park now requires permits to limit the (amount / number) of hikers on the mountain.

3. The rangers ask visitors to (comply to / comply with) the limits so that the cables near the summit don't become dangerously overcrowded with (to / too) many hikers.

4. The National Park Service installed the steel cables because the last 400 feet to the summit is (quiet / quite / quit) steep; with the cables, hikers can pull (themselves / theirselves) up the last section of the trail.

5. Despite the hike's popularity, this hike isn't for (every one / everyone) because of the sometimes (adverse / averse) conditions.

B Edit the following sentences to correct any misused words or idioms. Mark the one correct sentence "OK." (See 18c, 18d, the glossary of usage [p. 818] in *The Bedford Handbook*, Ninth Edition, or a dictionary if necessary.) Example:

             to hike
People who plan ~~on hiking~~ to Half Dome should be aware that the route is fourteen miles round trip.

6. Hikers must be sure and be in good physical shape to make the journey.

7. Water is not readily available along the route, so hikers must carry there own.

8. Conditions on the cable become dangerous during bad weather.

9. Rain can effect the cables, making them quite slippery.

10. According with park records, however, accidents on the cables are rare.

Van Goor and Hacker, *Developmental Exercises for The Bedford Handbook*, 9th ed. (Boston: Bedford, 2014)

18-3 | Exact words   **45**

EXERCISE 18-4 ◆ Exact words

To read about this topic, see section 18 in *The Bedford Handbook*, Ninth Edition.

Edit the following sentences to eliminate or replace clichés and to clarify mixed figures of speech. Mark the two correct sentences "OK." Example:

> **With more than four million annual visitors to Yosemite National Park, the park service**
>
> *manage the park carefully and wisely.*
> **must** ~~handle the park with kid gloves.~~
>   ^

1. The National Park Service continuously monitors the impact of visitors on every nook and cranny in Yosemite National Park.

2. At the end of the day, congestion in the park can diminish the quality of visitors' experiences.

3. As more and more vehicles enter the park, air and noise pollution increases by leaps and bounds.

4. The growing number of visitors can also result in destruction of park resources.

5. When visitors ignore signs and leave marked trails, delicate vegetation and animal habitats are here today and gone tomorrow.

6. Serious damage also results if everyone and his brother dig up rocks or build fires in unauthorized areas.

7. Last but not least, intentional acts such as vandalism cause serious, sometimes irreparable, damage.

8. One goal that is near and dear to the hearts of park service employees is to ensure a positive experience for all visitors to Yosemite National Park.

9. The National Park Service recognizes that human impact can result in negative experiences for all park visitors.

10. Park officials bend over backward to nip destructive activities in the bud to ensure that visitors have a pleasant experience.

Van Goor and Hacker, *Developmental Exercises for The Bedford Handbook,* 9th ed. (Boston: Bedford, 2014)

EXERCISE 18-5 ◆ Exact words: Guided review

Edit the following paragraph for language appropriate for an audience of educated nonexperts. The numbers in the margin refer to relevant rules in section 18 of *The Bedford Handbook*, Ninth Edition. The first revision has been done for you; find and correct the other six problems.

Yosemite National Park is home to more than four hundred animal species, but none seem to generate more interest and excitement among visitors ~~then~~ *than* the black bear. Park officials estimate that between three hundred and five hundred black bears live in the park, yet they generally keep their distance to humans. Spotting a bear is the best thing since sliced bread. Visitors should remember, however, that bears are wild, dangerous things. If a bear is spotted nearby, park rangers recommend keeping a distance of at least fifty yards. Should a bear attack, a rare event, visitors should never run; they should stand their ground, yell, and wave their arms to scare away the bear. When humans are careless, bears will loose their fear of humans. Some bears have learned that humans store food in their cars, and there have been reports of bears boldly entering campgrounds and breaking into vehicles to get at these tasty treats. It's better to be safe than sorry, so park regulations now require campers to keep their food in locked, bear-proof boxes, not in their tents or cars. Clearly, the best way to enjoy bear sightings is to keep bears in there natural habitat and humans in theirs.

18c

18d

18e

18b

18c

18e

18c

Van Goor and Hacker, *Developmental Exercises for The Bedford Handbook,* 9th ed. (Boston: Bedford, 2014)

18-5 | Exact words: Guided review **47**

REVIEW OF 16–18 ◆ Word choice

Edit the following essay to eliminate problems with word choice. The numbers in the margin refer to relevant rules in sections 16–18 of *The Bedford Handbook*, Ninth Edition. The first revision has been done for you.

Pristine wilderness, breathtaking vistas, and wild animals in their natural habitats lure over 275 million visitors ~~during a calendar year~~ annually to America's national parks. While the National Park Service puts forth effort toward the goal of protecting visitors by erecting safety barriers and enforcing safety rules, there are inherent dangers: fast-moving streams, high cliffs, rapidly changing weather conditions, and wildlife that is unpredictable. If visitors are unaware of these dangers, their carefree vacation can turn tragic.   16a

                                                                                                                                                                   16c

                                                                                                                                                                   16e

Annually, about 155 people meet the grim reaper in America's national parks. The greatest percentage of deaths is from drowning. After heavy winters, melting snow swells icy streams and creates powerful, fast-moving currents that put some boaters and swimmers into situations beyond their talents. Automobile accidents are the second most common cause of national park deaths. Things can easily distract drivers whose attention should be on the sometimes narrow two-lane roads. Falls account for the third highest percentage of park deaths. Visitors have climbed over safety fences, fallen over cliffs, and been swept over waterfalls. Climbers have slipped on loose or rain-slickened rocks and have fallen hundreds of feet to their deaths. Last but not least, animal attacks account for a very small percentage of national park fatalities; nevertheless, visitors have been killed due to the fact that they approached wildlife for that perfect photograph or because they surprised and inadvertently threatened a bear with cubs.   18a

                                                                                                                                                                   18c

                                                                                                                                                                   18b

                                                                                                                                                                   18e

                                                                                                                                                                   16c

Most of these tragic deaths could have been prevented. Park visitors should be sure and follow all safety rules and tips provided at park entrances. Safety fences and barriers should be heeded; visitors should never wade or swim upstream near waterfalls, nor should they swim in high water or whitewater conditions. Likewise, hikers should avoid ambulating close to river banks when the water is high.   18d

                                                                                                                                                                   17b

Van Goor and Hacker, Developmental Exercises for
The Bedford Handbook, 9th ed. (Boston: Bedford, 2014)

16–18 | Review: Word choice   **49**

Many tourists enter national parks under the false pretense that the parks

18c

are regulated and completely safe, as if they are amusement parks. Park employees

do what they can to protect clueless or complacent visitors, but it is up to the visitors

17d

themselves to understand the "wild" in wilderness.

Van Goor and Hacker, *Developmental Exercises for The Bedford Handbook,* 9th ed. (Boston: Bedford, 2014)

EXERCISE 19-1 ◆ Fragments: Guided practice

Edit the following paragraphs to eliminate sentence fragments. The numbers in the margin refer to relevant rules in section 19 of *The Bedford Handbook*, Ninth Edition. The first revision has been done for you; a suggested revision of this exercise appears in the back of this book.

        Four
~~How four~~ young Englishmen added a word to the world's vocabulary in the   19a

1960s. A word that became synonymous with the 1960s. Especially with the music of   19b, 19c

that time. That word was, of course, "Beatles." The Beatles became the most famous

popular musical group of the twentieth century. And have held the loyalty of many   19c

fans into the present century.

       The Beatles were popular in Liverpool, England, and in Hamburg, Germany.

Before they came to America on tour and became world famous. Liverpool and   19a

Hamburg loved the four young men and their music. The Beatles' favorite club was

the Cavern in Liverpool. Where they hung out together, played day and night, and   19a

attracted many fans. A Liverpool disc jockey first called attention to them, and a

Liverpool music critic and record store owner became their first manager. The disc

jockey called them "fantastic." Saying that they had "resurrected original rock 'n'   19b

roll." The music critic who became their manager, Brian Epstein, made them shape

up as a group. Promoting them, arranging club dates for them, and badgering record   19b

companies for them. He was determined to win a recording contract for this exciting

new group.

       In England, the record buying led to the publicity. In America, the publicity led

to the record buying. Everyone wanted copies of the original singles. "Love Me Do,"   19c

"Please, Please Me," and "From Me to You." In America, audiences made so much noise

that no one could hear the music. Crowds of screaming teenagers surrounded the

Beatles wherever they went. Determined to touch one or more of these famous music   19b

makers. Reporters observing the conduct of fans at Beatles' concerts found that they

had to invent a new word. To describe the wild, almost insane behavior of the fans.   19b

They called it "Beatlemania."

EXERCISE 19-2 ◆ Fragments

To read about this topic, see section 19 in *The Bedford Handbook*, Ninth Edition.

Each of the following word groups includes a subordinating word. One word group in each pair contains a fragment. Write "OK" after each item that does not contain a fragment and write "frag" after each item that contains a fragment. Example:

    a. **John Lennon lived with his Aunt Mimi until he was grown. Because his parents had separated and his mother had given John to Mimi.** *frag*

    b. **His father took him from Mimi when John was about five. Because his mother returned him to Mimi, he grew up as Mimi's child.** *OK*

1.   a.   When John Lennon was a teenager, his mother, Julia, began to pay more attention to his interests.

       b.   When Julia, John Lennon's mother, bought him a guitar and let him stay with her instead of his Aunt Mimi.

2.   a.   Although he studied art in college, he soon became more interested in music.

       b.   Although Julia encouraged his music and put up with the boyish pranks that annoyed Aunt Mimi.

3.   a.   His mother died before he was an adult. While John was still in college, in fact.

       b.   Mimi's husband, his uncle, had died while John still lived with them.

4.   a.   John asked Paul McCartney to join his group, and later Paul brought in George Harrison, and all three asked Ringo Starr to join them. Before they cut their first record.

       b.   In their early days, the Beatles copied people like Elvis Presley and Little Richard. Before these English boys even visited America, they sang with American accents.

5.   a.   The Beatles gave one reason for quitting their tours in 1966. That the tours were wrecking their playing.

       b.   Stopping the tours gave the Beatles an opportunity to expand their talents. That they learned to read musical notes and write their own music was key to their improvement as musicians.

Van Goor and Hacker, *Developmental Exercises for The Bedford Handbook*, 9th ed. (Boston: Bedford, 2014)

EXERCISE 19-3 ◆ Fragments

To read about this topic, see section 19 in *The Bedford Handbook*, Ninth Edition.

Underline each fragment in the following paragraphs. (Consult the chart on p. 279 of *The Bedford Handbook*, Ninth Edition, if necessary.) Do not correct the errors, but be prepared to discuss possible revision strategies for each fragment. The first fragment is underlined for you.

Paul McCartney wrote many of the Beatles' songs. A good student who learned quickly, he began composing songs when he was about fourteen.

Paul said that sometimes a song just came to him, like "Eleanor Rigby." <u>One of his most famous and moving songs.</u> The song is about a lonely woman who can't connect with other people. Paul was sitting at the piano not working on anything special. Just fooling around with melodies and rhythms. Then some notes played themselves in his head, and so did some words. Like "Daisy Hawkins picks up the rice in the church where a wedding has been." Later Paul saw the name "Rigby" on a shop in Bristol. And decided he liked that name better than "Hawkins," especially with "Eleanor" instead of "Daisy." He and John Lennon finished the song together.

Paul wrote "Hey, Jude" in an effort to help John's son, Julian, who was upset over his parents' separation. Paul wanted the boy not to be sad. "To take a sad song and make it better." He decided to change "Julian" to "Jude" after he finished the song. Because he wanted the song to have a country-and-western feel.

All of the Beatles wrote songs, and often they collaborated on one, but Paul McCartney and John Lennon wrote most of the songs the Beatles sang.

Van Goor and Hacker, *Developmental Exercises for The Bedford Handbook*, 9th ed. (Boston: Bedford, 2014)

19-3 | Fragments 53

EXERCISE 19-4 ◆ Fragments

To read about this topic, see section 19 in *The Bedford Handbook*, Ninth Edition.

Correct the fragments in the following paragraphs. The first revision has been done for you. Find and revise ten more fragments.

George Harrison was known in school for two things ✏️ ~~His~~ *his* sharp clothes and his love of the guitar. His mother said he sometimes practiced the guitar for hours. Not stopping until his fingers were bleeding. When George met John Lennon, he found another guitar lover. Although they went to the same school, they did not meet there. Because George was two years younger and they had no classes together. Instead, they met on the school bus. After they became friends, they spent most of their time at George's house, playing their guitars.

When George, John, Paul McCartney, and Ringo Starr formed a group, the four experimented with all kinds of things. From melodies and sounds to drugs. George, however, began to want more out of life. To find answers to the big questions he had about war and loneliness and reasons for living. The others agreed to search with him, and George Harrison became their guide.

Later, George and his wife went to India. Where a religious festival they attended impressed them deeply. When George returned to England, he read many books about meditation. And went to hear Indian holy teachers. He shared what he read and heard with the other Beatles. Who were just as interested as George was. When George learned that a holy man called the Maharishi was going to speak on transcendental meditation, he told his friends. They all went to listen to him. To learn whatever they could that would help them.

The Beatles were headed in a new direction. A direction that was obvious in their next album, *Sgt. Pepper's Lonely Hearts Club Band*. The album had innovative lyrics and an amazing musical background. A forty-one-piece orchestra, guitar, sitar, doubled voices, a comb-and-paper instrument, and all kinds of electronic and percussion tricks. The Beatles were no longer copycat rock and rollers.

Van Goor and Hacker, *Developmental Exercises for The Bedford Handbook*, 9th ed. (Boston: Bedford, 2014)

EXERCISE 19-5 ◆ Fragments

To read about this topic, see section 19 in *The Bedford Handbook*, Ninth Edition.

Half of the following word groups are complete sentences. The other half contain fragments. Correct the fragments, and mark the complete sentences "OK." Example:

> As a child and a teenager, Ringo Starr spent a total of three years in the hospital/~~Because~~ *because* of two severe health problems.

1. When Ringo Starr was six, a burst appendix put him in the hospital for a whole year. Because of problems the rupture caused.

2. His doctors had to perform several operations; Ringo could not attend school at all that year.

3. His babysitter taught him to read and write, so he did not fall too far behind in his schoolwork.

4. When he was thirteen, Ringo had to go back into the hospital. And stay there for two years while doctors treated a lung condition.

5. At age fifteen, he worked at various jobs. But what he really liked best was playing the drums for his many fans.

6. Having taught himself on drums he bought on the installment plan, he played with different musical groups in Liverpool, including the Beatles.

7. When Ringo joined the Beatles, not everyone was sure that he could handle the job. For example, George Martin, a record producer who invited them to London to record an album.

8. Martin insisted on a standby drummer as insurance. Someone ready to step in just in case Ringo was not good enough.

9. Ringo's many devoted fans were not surprised when he handled the job and became a full-fledged Beatle, making new friends at every engagement.

10. Many people considered him the most likable member of the group. Because of his easy smile and his open approach to life.

Van Goor and Hacker, *Developmental Exercises for The Bedford Handbook*, 9th ed. (Boston: Bedford, 2014)

19-5 | Fragments   55

EXERCISE 19-6 ◆ Fragments: Guided review

Find and correct the sentence fragments in the following paragraphs. The numbers in the margin refer to relevant rules in section 19 of *The Bedford Handbook*, Ninth Edition. The first revision has been done for you.

Many people influenced the Beatles in their career. For example, Bob Waller, a disc jockey in Liverpool/, ~~He~~ first called attention to them in one of his articles. **19c**

"They resurrected original rock 'n' roll," he wrote. When he first heard them in 1961. **19a**

From Stu Sutcliffe, a talented musician who sometimes played with them, the Beatles copied several things. Their hairstyle, their dress, and much of their philosophy. **19c**

George Martin, who produced their records, advised them how to improve after their early records. And taught them how to use tapes. **19c**

The person who influenced them most, however, was Brian Epstein. Owner of **19b** several record stores and reviewer of new records. When a customer asked for a record by a group Epstein had never heard of, he went from club to club. Looking for a group **19b** calling itself "The Beatles." By the end of 1961, he had become the group's manager. Convinced that he had found talented and original musicians. His contract said that **19b** he was to promote the Beatles and arrange their tours and club dates. His other duty was really the most important. To get record contracts for them. **19b**

Epstein did far more than his contract called for. He made the young men wear suits every time they performed. Until their gray, collarless outfits became a symbol of **19a** the Beatles. He made another demand of them. That they be on time for appearances. **19a** He even made them quit chewing gum onstage. And by the time he had done all these things, he had also gotten them a recording date. Why were the Beatles so devastated by Epstein's death? When Brian Epstein was found dead of an accidental drug **19a** overdose in 1967. The Beatles lost far more than a good manager. They lost a close friend and mentor.

Van Goor and Hacker, *Developmental Exercises for The Bedford Handbook*, 9th ed. (Boston: Bedford, 2014)

EXERCISE 20-1 ◆ Run-on sentences: Guided practice

Edit the following paragraphs to eliminate run-on sentences. Each number in the margin indicates a problem in that line and refers to a relevant rule in section 20 of *The Bedford Handbook*, Ninth Edition. The first revision has been done for you; a suggested revision of this exercise appears in the back of this book.

             Not

Have you ever heard of the Wobblies~~/? not~~ many people have these days. That's   20c

a shame they did at least two things for which they should be remembered. They   20d

probably saved the labor movement in America, they definitely gave American folk   20a

music some of its most unforgettable songs. No one really knows how they got their

nickname almost everyone knows a song or two that they inspired.   20a

   The Wobblies were the members of the Industrial Workers of the World (IWW),

this union was a small but militant coalition of radical labor groups. The Wobblies   20d

could not get along with the major union groups of the day, in fact, they alienated most   20b

of those groups.

   The major unions disliked the Wobblies immensely, nevertheless they learned   20d

some valuable lessons from them. The first lesson was to avoid getting involved

in politics. If there was one thing the Wobblies hated more than capitalism, it was

politics. The Wobblies avoided politics for one good reason, they believed that political   20b

affiliation caused the death of unions. What else did the major unions learn, they   20c

learned to deal realistically with workers' problems. Major unions also learned new

recruiting techniques from the Wobblies. In addition, they copied the Wobblies in

devoting their energy to nuts-and-bolts issues affecting the workers.

   The major unions never recognized their debt to the Wobblies, the debt was still   20a

there for historians to see. Historians began to compile the story of the American labor

unions, then they finally recognized the contributions of the Wobblies.   20d

EXERCISE 20-2 ◆ Run-on sentences

To read about this topic, see section 20 in *The Bedford Handbook*, Ninth Edition.

One sentence in each of the following pairs is a run-on sentence. Find and correct the error, using an effective revision strategy. Mark the correct sentence "OK." Example:

    Although
  a. Joe Hill may not have been the first martyr of the labor movement, ~~however,~~ he was certainly its most skillful worker with words and music.

  b. Before his arrest in 1914 for killing a grocer in Salt Lake City, Joe Hill was simply the Swedish immigrant Joseph Hillstrom; no one knew or cared much about him. *OK*

1. a. Ralph Chaplin was the only person who wrote anything about Joe Hill before Hill's execution, he jotted down just a few notes based on an interview with a drunken sailor.

    b. Extensive historical research has not confirmed or denied those notes because researchers have turned up quite different stories.

2. a. All the evidence introduced at Hill's trial was circumstantial; furthermore, the dead man's son, who had witnessed the murder, refused to identify Hill as the gunman.

    b. Did the state hide evidence it certainly seemed that way.

3. a. One Wobbly told the police that he had been with Joe Hill in another location on the night of the murder, he also told a detective he could prove Hill's innocence.

    b. That man was promptly arrested and held in jail for the duration of the trial.

4. a. At the end of the trial, the man was released and ordered to leave the state.

    b. Hill's own attorneys did not do much to help him their attitude was as negative as that of the prosecutors.

5. a. Because of their negative attitude, Hill discharged both of the attorneys who were supposed to be defending him.

    b. "I have three prosecutors here, I intend to get rid of two of them," he said.

Van Goor and Hacker, *Developmental Exercises for
The Bedford Handbook*, 9th ed. (Boston: Bedford, 2014)

20-2 | Run-on sentences **59**

6.   a.   The state never showed a motive for the murder; furthermore, much evidence that Hill's attorneys could have used was never introduced.

      b.   How did Hill get that bullet wound in his chest, he told the doctor he had gotten it in a fight over a woman.

7.   a.   The doctor who treated Hill was not asked to testify about medical aspects of the case, as a matter of fact, his testimony probably would have prevented Hill's conviction.

      b.   Protests about Hill's conviction came from all over the world, but they were ignored.

8.   a.   Important political figures tried to help Hill, hoping until the last minute that they could save him.

      b.   The Swedish consul pleaded for him, President Wilson sent telegrams to the governor of Utah.

9.   a.   Legend has it that Hill's last words before the firing squad were "Don't mourn for me; organize," in fact, he said, "Yes, aim! Let her go! Fire!"

      b.   If Joe Hill is known at all today, it is probably because of Joe Glazer, his guitar, and the song "Joe Hill."

10.   a.   Glazer was not the composer of "Joe Hill" its composers were Earl Robinson and Alfred Hayes.

      b.   Glazer, however, made the song known across America, singing it at banquets as well as on picket lines.

Van Goor and Hacker, *Developmental Exercises for The Bedford Handbook,* 9th ed. (Boston: Bedford, 2014)

EXERCISE 20-3 ◆ Run-on sentences

To read about this topic, see section 20 in *The Bedford Handbook*, Ninth Edition.

Correct each run-on sentence using the method of revision suggested in brackets. Example:

> *with whom*
> **From his death cell, Joe Hill sent a letter to Big Bill Haywood, he had worked ~~with~~**
>
> **~~Haywood~~ in the early days of the IWW. [Restructure the sentence; see 20d.]**

1. Joe Hill's final letter to Big Bill Haywood had only five sentences, it contained one line about his death, one admonition to Haywood, and three comments related to Hill's burial. [Use a colon; see 20b.]

2. He commented briefly about his death he said, "I die like a true rebel." [Restructure the sentence; see 20d.]

3. Hill told Haywood, "Don't waste time mourning for me, organize instead." [Use a semicolon; see 20b.]

4. Hill, in prison in Utah, did not want to be buried in that state, he asked Haywood to haul his body into Wyoming, a hundred miles away. [Use a coordinating conjunction; see 20a.]

5. Hill gave only one reason for requesting burial in Wyoming, he said, "I don't want to be found dead in Utah." [Make two sentences; see 20c.]

6. On the night before his execution, he wrote a final poem, in it he made two requests. [Restructure the sentence; see 20d.]

7. He wanted his body to be cremated, he wanted his ashes to be allowed to blow freely around the earth. [Use a coordinating conjunction; see 20a.]

8. Here's how he said it in his poem,

   > Let the merry breezes blow
   > My dust to where some flowers grow.
   > Perhaps some fading flower then
   > Would come to life and bloom again. [Use a colon; see 20b.]

9. Obviously, Joe Hill was not a great poet, however, he was clever with rhymes. [Use a semicolon; see 20b.]

10. Even in his will he managed to fit in a humorous rhyme,

    > This is my last and final will.
    > Good luck to all of you.
    > —Joe Hill [Use a colon; see 20b.]

Van Goor and Hacker, *Developmental Exercises for*
The Bedford Handbook, 9th ed. (Boston: Bedford, 2014)

20-3 | Run-on sentences   **61**

EXERCISE 20-4 ◆ Run-on sentences

To read about this topic, see section 20 in *The Bedford Handbook*, Ninth Edition.

Correct each of the following run-on sentences in the way you think is most effective. Example:

Joe Hill was not buried in Utah ; he was not buried in Wyoming either.

1. After Joe Hill's death, his body was sent to Chicago, a large auditorium was secured for the funeral services.

2. More than thirty thousand people overflowed the auditorium, they jammed the streets as they followed the funeral train to the cemetery.

3. Very few of these mourners knew Joe Hill personally, nevertheless, he was a true hero to them.

4. On that Thanksgiving Day of 1915, they knew that other people mourned him too they heard eulogies to him in nine different languages.

5. Those mourners and thousands like them sang his songs, because they did, Joe Hill's name lived on.

6. Hill's satirical, angry songs often had a surprising tenderness, it is no wonder that he was named poet laureate of the Wobbly movement.

7. In some ways, Joe Hill's death freed him, in other ways, he remains a prisoner.

8. Joe Hill did get part of his deathbed wish, his body was cremated.

9. He was cremated at the cemetery afterward his ashes were put in thirty envelopes and sent all over the world.

10. The IWW kept one envelope, the Department of Justice confiscated it in 1918 for use in a trial. Since the envelope was never returned, part of Joe Hill is still "in prison."

Van Goor and Hacker, *Developmental Exercises for The Bedford Handbook*, 9th ed. (Boston: Bedford, 2014)

EXERCISE 20-5 ◆ Run-on sentences: Guided review

Revise each run-on sentence in the following paragraphs using the method suggested by the rule noted in the margin. See section 20 of *The Bedford Handbook*, Ninth Edition. The first sentence has been revised for you.

Although he
~~He~~ never calls them by name, John Steinbeck immortalizes the Wobblies in ⟨20d⟩

The Grapes of Wrath. The novel is about the life of the Joad family. The Joads have ⟨20d⟩

lost their farm during the Depression, the family has come to California seeking work.

There is no permanent work for anyone, moreover, the money earned by picking crops ⟨20b⟩

is not enough to feed the family.

Union organizers have talked to the workers about organizing and striking.

Tom, the oldest Joad son, has listened to them, however, he has not yet joined them. ⟨20a⟩

Tom is in hiding because he has accidentally killed a man in a fight. He spends all

his daylight hours alone, he has lots of time to think about his family's situation. Tom ⟨20a⟩

becomes convinced that life is unfair for his people, he decides to leave the family, find ⟨20d⟩

the union men, and work with them.

He is inarticulate when he tries to explain to Ma what he hopes to do he ⟨20c⟩

gropes for words to express his frustration and his hope. Ma asks him how she will

know about him, she worries that he might get killed and she would not know. Tom's ⟨20a⟩

reassurances are almost mystical: "Wherever they's a fight so hungry people can eat,

I'll be there. . . . An' when our folks eat the stuff they raise an' live in the houses they

build—why, I'll be there."

If Tom had had a copy of the Wobblies' "little red song book," he could have

found less mystical words. Every copy of the book contained the Wobblies' Preamble,

the first sentence in the Preamble was unmistakably clear "The working class and the ⟨20d, 20b⟩

employing class have nothing in common." Tom would have understood those words he ⟨20b⟩

would have believed them, too.

Van Goor and Hacker, *Developmental Exercises for*
The Bedford Handbook, 9th ed. (Boston: Bedford, 2014)

20-5 | Run-on sentences: Guided review **63**

EXERCISE 21-1 ◆ Subject-verb agreement: Guided practice

Circle the correct verb from each pair in parentheses. The numbers in the margin refer to relevant rules in section 21 of *The Bedford Handbook*, Ninth Edition. The first selection has been made for you; answers to this exercise appear in the back of this book.

Before reaching college, nearly everyone already (knows / know) several facts   21e

about fables. Most students know, for example, that fables are short stories that

(conveys / convey) a moral. They also know that fables nearly always have animal   21i

characters but that animal characters alone (is / are) not a signal that the story is a   21h

fable. They know of Aesop, to whom most familiar fables in Western culture (is / are)   21b

attributed. They know that there (is / are) generally only two or three characters in   21g

an Aesop fable and that a crowd of observers almost never (has / have) a role in his   21f

stories.

Most adults recognize that the subject matter of Aesop's fables is nearly always

the same. Once in a while, but not often, politics (is / are) highlighted in a story.   21j

Usually, however, Aesop's fables point out the value of common sense or make gentle

fun of human failings. Since neither foolish behavior nor human failings

(seems / seem) to be in short supply, Aesop's stories continue to be told. Besides, they   21d

attract a wide audience: Adults and children both (enjoy / enjoys) them. Everyone who   21c

has gone to school (is / are) supposed to know some of Aesop's fables. "The Fox and the   21e

Grapes," for instance, (is / are) familiar to many children as a story long before they   21k

understand its meaning.

Van Goor and Hacker, *Developmental Exercises for The Bedford Handbook*, 9th ed. (Boston: Bedford, 2014)

EXERCISE 21-2 ◆ Subject-verb agreement

To read about this topic, see section 21 in *The Bedford Handbook*, Ninth Edition.

Verbs in the following sentences are italicized. Underline the simple subject (or simple subjects) of each verb, and edit the verb to make it agree with the subject. Keep all verbs in the present tense. Do not change the three correct sentences. Example:

> *have*
> <u>Many</u> of the morals or wise sayings from fables ~~has~~ become a part of our language.
> ^

1. Phrases like "a wolf in sheep's clothing" *is used and understood* by many people.

2. The expression "a wolf in sheep's clothing" *comes* from one of Aesop's fables.

3. A flock of sheep and a hungry wolf *is* the main characters in the story.

4. After killing a sheep for their supper, the shepherd and his helpers *forgets* about the skin from the sheep.

5. The wolf, finding the discarded skin, *cover* himself with it.

6. Joining the flock, he *pretends* to be a mother looking for her lamb.

7. The flock *accept* him as a sheep.

8. Neither the sheep nor the shepherd *notice* the wolf at first.

9. Luring a lamb from the flock each day, the wolf *feeds* himself very well for a while.

10. Everyone hearing the story *understand* its warning: to beware of people pretending to be what they are not.

Van Goor and Hacker, *Developmental Exercises for*
The Bedford Handbook, 9th ed. (Boston: Bedford, 2014)

21-2 | Subject-verb agreement **65**

EXERCISE 21-3 ◆ Subject-verb agreement

To read about this topic, see section 21 in *The Bedford Handbook*, Ninth Edition.

Each of the following sentences has two subjects and verbs (some of the subject-verb pairs are in subordinate structures). The simple subjects are italicized. Edit each incorrect verb to make it agree with its subject. Keep all verbs in the present tense. One subject-verb pair in each sentence is correct. Example:

is
"Sour grapes" ~~are~~ a common expression, but not *everyone* knows the origin of that phrase.
^

1. Aesop's *story* "The Fox and the Grapes" tells about a fox *who* try unsuccessfully to get some grapes.

2. There are a big *bunch* of grapes hanging over the top of a wall, and the *fox* is hot and thirsty.

3. A favorite *food* of his are grapes, and *he* leaps up to get some—without success.

4. Hoping that no *crowd* of friends are watching, the *fox* takes a running leap for the top of the wall.

5. Unsuccessful, the *fox* in the story tries again and again with the same result; neither his *cleverness* nor his high *leaps* is successful.

6. Embarrassed, the *fox* fears that *news* of his failures are going to give his friends something to tease him about.

7. The fox's *pride* and his *self-confidence* has suffered, so *he* claims not to want the grapes anyway.

8. The *fox*, stalking proudly off with his nose in the air, say that the *grapes* are sour.

9. *Everyone* know that the *fox* does not believe his own words.

10. To save their pride, *people* often pretends not to want what *they* cannot get.

Van Goor and Hacker, *Developmental Exercises for The Bedford Handbook*, 9th ed. (Boston: Bedford, 2014)

EXERCISE 21-4 ◆ Subject-verb agreement: Guided review

Circle the correct verb from each pair in parentheses. The numbers in the margin refer to relevant rules in section 21 of *The Bedford Handbook*, Ninth Edition. The first selection has been made for you.

From one of Aesop's lesser-known fables (comes / come) the question "Who's   21g

going to bell the cat?" The fable "Belling the Cat" describes the long battle between

mice and cats.

In the story, a committee of mice is appointed to find a way to keep the cat from

killing so many mice. Everyone on the committee (tries / try) to solve the problem.   21e

There (is / are) many committee meetings and much discussion, but in the end neither   21g

the committee nor its chairperson (is / are) able to make any good suggestions. Finally,   21d

the time comes for the committee to make its report at a public meeting. Embarrassed,

the committee (reports / report) its failure.   21f

At first, there is only silence; no one wants to accept the committee's report as

the final word on the problem. Then a little pip-squeak among the mice (suggests /   21b

suggest) tying a bell on the cat. The young mouse makes quite a speech in favor of his

idea. According to that mouse, statistics (shows / show) that no mice have ever been   21j

captured by a noisy cat. The mouse points out that his solution would not cost much;

a bell and a string (is / are) all the equipment needed to give the mice warning of the   21c

cat's approach. The mouse who makes the suggestion gets a round of applause. The

committee members, who (wishes / wish) that they had thought of the idea, are silent.   21i

Then a wise old mouse asks, "Who will bell the cat?" The experienced mice and the

young pip-squeak (is / are) silent.   21c

It is easy to make suggestions that other people (has / have) to carry out.   21a

EXERCISE 22-1 ◆ Pronoun-antecedent agreement: Guided practice

Edit the following paragraphs for problems with pronoun-antecedent agreement. The numbers in the margin refer to relevant rules in section 22 of *The Bedford Handbook*, Ninth Edition. The first revision has been done for you; a suggested revision of this exercise appears in the back of this book.

Everyone has heard of Dorothy and Toto and their tornado "flight" from Kansas

Everyone also knows

to Oz. ~~They also know~~ that the Oz adventure was pure fantasy and that it ended   22a

happily. But another girl from Kansas took real flights all around the real world.

Whenever she landed safely after setting one of her many records, everyone rejoiced

and sent their congratulations to her. When she disappeared on her last flight, the   22a

whole world mourned. Not every pilot can claim they have that kind of following.   22a

Neighbors knew that Amelia Earhart would not be a typical "lady." A child as

curious, daring, and self-confident as Amelia was bound to stand out from her peers.

When she and her sister Muriel were young, girls were supposed to play with dolls. If

a girl played baseball or collected worms, they were called "tomboys" and were often   22a

punished. Boys and girls even had different kinds of sleds—the girls' sleds were

lightweight, impossible-to-steer box sleds.

But the Earhart family lived by their own rules. Amelia's father, whom she   22b

depended on for approval, bought Amelia the boys' sled she longed for. Many fast trips

down steep hills gave Amelia a foretaste of flying with the wind in her face.

The closest Amelia came to flying was on a homemade roller coaster. She and

her friends built it, using an old woodshed for the base of the ride. They started eight

feet off the ground and tried to sled down the slope without falling off. No one was

successful on their first attempt, but Amelia kept trying until she had a successful   22a

ride. Satisfied at last, she declared that the ride had felt "just like flying."

Van Goor and Hacker, *Developmental Exercises for The Bedford Handbook*, 9th ed. (Boston: Bedford, 2014)

EXERCISE 22-2 ◆ Pronoun-antecedent agreement

To read about this topic, see section 22 in *The Bedford Handbook*, Ninth Edition.

Five of the following word groups contain a problem with pronoun-antecedent agreement. Mark the correct word groups "OK" and edit the incorrect ones to eliminate the problem. Example:

> During World War I, Amelia Earhart listened to wounded pilots' tales of adventure. ~~A pilot~~ *Pilots* would describe a particularly daring wartime adventure and joke about their ability to beat the odds.

1. After World War I, Amelia Earhart took flying lessons. She learned quickly, but the lessons cost her most of her salary.

2. She wanted those lessons, so she worked two jobs to pay for them: She clerked for the telephone company and drove a dump truck for a sand and gravel company.

3. Members of her family pooled their funds to buy a gift—a little yellow biplane—for her twenty-fourth birthday celebration; it was the perfect gift.

4. Amelia Earhart soon learned that when someone owns a plane, they need a lot of money.

5. She sometimes executed dangerous maneuvers before her teacher was sure Amelia could handle it.

6. At first everyone could not believe their eyes when she deliberately put her plane into a spin.

7. Each spectator would gasp when they heard her cut the engine off in a spin.

8. But Amelia Earhart repeatedly pulled the plane out of its spin and landed safely, delighting everyone.

9. When an aviator wants to break records, they will work very hard.

10. Aviation record keepers had to make a new entry in the record books: They had seen Amelia Earhart fly 14,000 feet high.

Van Goor and Hacker, *Developmental Exercises for The Bedford Handbook*, 9th ed. (Boston: Bedford, 2014)

22-2 | Pronoun-antecedent agreement **69**

EXERCISE 22-3 ◆ Pronoun-antecedent agreement

To read about this topic, see section 22 in *The Bedford Handbook*, Ninth Edition.

In each set of sentences, circle the letter of the sentence that has a problem with pronoun-antecedent agreement. Which of the other two sentences (both correct) do you prefer? Put a check mark next to that sentence. Example:

> **(a.)** A college dropout often gets little respect for their choosing to leave school.
>
> **b.** College dropouts often get little respect for their choosing to leave school.
>
> ✔ **c.** A college dropout often gets little respect for choosing to leave school.

1. a. Not everyone who drops out of college ruins their life.

    b. Not all students who drop out of college ruin their lives.

    c. Not all college dropouts ruin their lives.

2. a. Students sometimes discover that they don't like their chosen field.

    b. A student sometimes discovers that he or she doesn't like their chosen field.

    c. Students may lose interest in their chosen field.

3. a. People like Amelia, who quit school to learn to fly, must be very sure of themselves.

    b. Someone like Amelia, who quit school to learn to fly, must be very sure of themselves.

    c. Someone like Amelia, who quit school to learn to fly, must be very sure of herself or himself.

4. a. In their catalog, Columbia University offered a wide range of courses, but Flying Airplanes was not among them.

    b. Flying Airplanes was not among the wide range of courses offered in Columbia University's catalog.

    c. In its catalog, Columbia University offered a wide range of courses, but Flying Airplanes was not among them.

5. a. Amelia Earhart became a dropout any university would be proud to claim.

    b. Amelia Earhart became one of those dropouts any university would be proud to claim as theirs.

    c. Amelia Earhart became a dropout all universities would be proud to claim.

Van Goor and Hacker, *Developmental Exercises for*
The Bedford Handbook, 9th ed. (Boston: Bedford, 2014)

EXERCISE 22-4 ◆ Pronoun-antecedent agreement: Guided review

Edit the following paragraphs for problems with pronoun-antecedent agreement. The numbers in the margin refer to relevant rules in section 22 of *The Bedford Handbook*, Ninth Edition. The first revision has been done for you.

When Amelia Earhart became the first woman to cross the Atlantic in a plane,

she got no money; she did get a free ride, fame, and job offers. Not ~~every flier~~ *all fliers* would   22a

think these rewards were enough for their time and trouble on the trip, but Amelia

Earhart was delighted with the whole experience. Afterward, a book she wrote about

that flight brought her another first: a publisher, a shrewd business manager, and

a husband—all in one man, George Putnam. (Putnam also understood her fierce

independence—not every man would sign a prenuptial agreement saying that their   22a

wife could have a divorce anytime she asked!)

The first national organization for "flying women," formed by Amelia Earhart

and a friend, recruited their members in the belief that every woman should follow   22b

her own interest. After all, who had made the first solo flight from Honolulu to the

United States? From Los Angeles to Mexico City? And from Mexico City to New

Jersey? It was she, Amelia Earhart. No woman ever did more to prove that they could   22a

handle jobs traditionally reserved for men.

Amelia Earhart's last "first" was never completed. When she tried to become the

first pilot to fly around the world at the equator, she disappeared somewhere over the

Pacific. The US government search covered more than 265,000 miles of air and sea

space, but they found nothing.   22a

In 1994, fifty-seven years after Amelia Earhart's disappearance, twelve-year-old

Vicki Van Meter became the youngest female pilot to fly across the Atlantic. She took

off from Augusta, Maine, from the very spot where Amelia Earhart had started her

flight across the Atlantic. When Van Meter landed safely in Glasgow, everyone offered

their congratulations, and Van Meter felt a special kinship with her predecessor,   22a

Amelia Earhart.

EXERCISE 23-1 ◆ Pronoun reference: Guided practice

Edit the following paragraphs to correct errors in pronoun reference. The numbers in the margin refer to relevant rules in section 23 of *The Bedford Handbook*, Ninth Edition. The first revision has been done for you; a suggested revision of this exercise appears in the back of this book.

George and Mary Jones lived in Memphis during the Civil War. They were

Being caught in the middle

sympathetic to the Union, but the city definitely favored the Confederates. ~~This~~ made   23b

the war years especially hard on them. They looked forward to a much better life after

the war.

At first, it seemed that they were going to have that better life. George got a job

as a labor organizer, and Mary stayed at home to care for their four healthy children.

Then came yellow fever. In nine months, Mary went from a happy wife and mother to

a despondent widow with no children. She had to find work. Because you must have   23d

some meaning for living, she needed work that she could care strongly about.

By 1900, Mary had become involved in union activities all over the United

States. She found her calling among the coal miners and their wives, which she   23a

followed for the next thirty years. Making friends with the workers and outwitting

private detectives, she held secret meetings to help them organize and plan strategy.   23a

In the newspaper, it often reported her ability to outwit and outlast mine bosses and   23d

lawyers as well as to reawaken courage in disconsolate workers.

Mary Jones spent many nights in jail, but often her jailers did not know what

to do with this attractive gray-haired woman whom the workers called "Mother." The

jailers' confusion simply amused Mary, who was far more used to jail than they could   23c

imagine.

Van Goor and Hacker, *Developmental Exercises for
The Bedford Handbook,* 9th ed. (Boston: Bedford, 2014)

EXERCISE 23-2 ◆ Pronoun reference

To read about this topic, see section 23 in *The Bedford Handbook*, Ninth Edition.

Six of the following sentences contain faulty pronoun references. Find the faulty references and fix them. Mark the correct sentences "OK." Example:

> *and this job*
> Mother Jones got a job working in the textile mills, ~~which~~ made her conscious of how
> women workers were mistreated.

1. When Mother Jones started working in the textile mills at the turn of the twentieth century, she saw "the little gray ghosts," the child laborers which worked from sunup to sundown.

2. Children as young as six scooted along the floor oiling and cleaning the huge whirring looms, which often devoured a child's fingers or hand.

3. Mother Jones once led a delegation of three hundred children from Philadelphia to New York to dramatize their plight; in some of the newspapers, they called her "the greatest female agitator in the country."

4. The speeches Mother Jones made about child labor were among her best: They called for legislation to forbid labor practices dangerous to children's health.

5. When Mother Jones asked for permission to bring three of the children to meet with President Theodore Roosevelt in New York, she was refused. It saddened her because she had hoped for the president's help.

6. Mother Jones asked again and was again refused. This second one saddened her even more, but she still did not consider the trip a failure.

7. She told the children and their parents that they had been successful.

8. Public awareness, which she felt would help the children, gradually began to increase.

9. Thousands of people had learned about the children's plight, which was bound to affect their thinking about child labor laws.

10. Mother Jones's optimism had another basis as well: The children would remember—and they would grow up.

Van Goor and Hacker, *Developmental Exercises for*
The Bedford Handbook, 9th ed. (Boston: Bedford, 2014)

23-2 | Pronoun reference **73**

EXERCISE 23-3 ◆ Pronoun reference

To read about this topic, see section 23 in *The Bedford Handbook*, Ninth Edition.

Problem pronouns are italicized in the following paragraphs. Edit the paragraphs to eliminate any misunderstandings these pronouns might cause. You may need to restructure some sentences. Example:

> *workers*
> In the mines, ~~you~~ didn't get much chance at the good life.

Mother Jones was determined to change the intolerable working conditions in the mines. After digging coal in twelve-to-fourteen-hour shifts, *they* found in their miners' pay envelopes not US currency but scrip, paper money that was honored only by the mining company. Local merchants had no use for the scrip, so *they* couldn't use it to buy food, clothes, or anything else. Workers, therefore, had to rent their homes from the company and buy their supplies at company stores. In company-run schools, the workers' children were taught by teachers *that* were hired by the company. *Their* families listened to company-paid ministers in company-owned churches.

Songwriter Merle Travis may have broken a pronoun reference rule, but he certainly summed *it* up neatly in one of his songs:

You load sixteen tons, what do you get?

Another day older and deeper in debt.

St. Peter, don't you call me 'cause I can't go.

I owe my soul to the company store.

[What pronoun does Travis use in a way that would be inappropriate in formal written English?]

Van Goor and Hacker, *Developmental Exercises for The Bedford Handbook*, 9th ed. (Boston: Bedford, 2014)

EXERCISE 23-4 ◆ Pronoun reference: Guided review

Edit the following paragraphs to correct errors in pronoun reference. The numbers in the margin refer to relevant rules in section 23 of *The Bedford Handbook*, Ninth Edition. The first revision has been done for you.

Coal miners' struggles turned into actual war in the Kanawha Valley of West
Virginia, where ~~they~~ *miners* were striking. The mine owners dominated the courts and the   23c
newspapers; they did not need to worry about the law or public opinion. Although
the miners did not want to accept this, they were often forced to face it. Guards   23b
used violent tactics to maintain the mine owners' control, once spraying strikers'
tent colonies with machine-gun fire and kicking a pregnant woman so hard that her
unborn child died in the womb.

Mother Jones urged the miners to fight while she tried to gain the ear of the
governor, federal lawmakers, and the public. In records of the fight, it says that two   23d
thousand miners came from outside the valley to help in the battle. The state militia
was called in, but the owners got control of the militia soon after it arrived. En route
to the state legislature to ask them for help, Mother Jones was kidnapped by soldiers,   23c
held incommunicado, put in solitary confinement, and tried by a military court. When
the new governor of West Virginia, Henry D. Hatfield, investigated, he found a soldier
guarding an eighty-year-old pneumonia-ridden woman that had a 104-degree fever.   23e

Word about the Kanawha situation got out, but Governor Hatfield acted first.
Out of his work came the Hatfield Agreement. This document, which historians of the
labor movement consider a major advance for workers in the United States, forced the
companies to recognize the union and to shorten the workday. Even more important,
it stipulated that companies must pay wages in US currency. He also guaranteed   23a
civilians the right to civil, not military, trials and dismissed all sentences the military
court had imposed—including the twenty-year prison term it had set for Mother
Jones.

Van Goor and Hacker, *Developmental Exercises for*
The Bedford Handbook, 9th ed. (Boston: Bedford, 2014)

23-4 | Pronoun reference: Guided review   **75**

EXERCISE 24-1 ◆ Pronoun and noun case: Guided practice

Circle the correct pronoun or noun from each pair of words in parentheses. The numbers in the margin refer to relevant rules in section 24 of *The Bedford Handbook*, Ninth Edition. The first selection has been made for you; answers to this exercise appear in the back of this book.

When union organizer Mother Jones went to Colorado in 1913, no one worked

harder than (she/ her) to help the miners. (They / Them) and their families lived in   24d, 24a

company houses that the company's own reports called unfit for human habitation.

Although Mother Jones wanted to help the miners, she saw no way to get the two

groups, the owners and (they / them), together.   24c

Mother Jones did not give up. When threatening posters went up all over town,

she laughed and encouraged the miners with slogans like "(We / Us) miners have got   24e

to stick together." When Mother Jones appealed to the governor for help, no one really

expected the governor and (she / her) to agree, but many people hoped he would help   24f

somehow. Instead, he simply ordered her out of the state.

The miners were evicted from their houses. (They / Them) and their families   24a

moved into tents. After company guards raked the tents with machine-gun fire, the

miners dug pits under the tents. The pits were deep enough to protect their families

and (they / them) from gunfire, but at Ludlow, guards set fire to the tents. Whole   24b

families were roasted to death in the pits. When word of the massacre got out, workers

from all over the state swarmed to Ludlow. No one was ever as angry as (they / them).   24d

They set fire to company buildings, fought the state and company troops, and took

over the nearby mines and towns.

Mother Jones went to Washington to ask President Wilson for help. Although

she and (he / him) did not agree on all points, he did establish a review board and   24a

send in federal troops to restore order. The companies did not like the (president /   24g

president's) sending in troops and absolutely refused to accept the findings of the

review board. Eventually, the miners went back to work under almost the same

conditions as before. Disappointed as they were, they knew that it was (she / her),   24a

Mother Jones, who was the most disappointed of all.

Van Goor and Hacker, *Developmental Exercises for
The Bedford Handbook,* 9th ed. (Boston: Bedford, 2014)

EXERCISE 24-2 ◆ Pronoun and noun case

To read about this topic, see section 24 in *The Bedford Handbook*, Ninth Edition.

Six of the following sentences have errors in pronoun or noun case. Find and fix the errors. Mark "OK" next to the sentences that have no errors. Example:

> *he*
> **Mother Jones liked to discuss union affairs with her friend Terence Powderly; she and ~~him~~**
>   ^
> **could argue for hours about the best approach to a problem.**

1. People all over the world knew about Mother Jones. Wherever she went, she was invited into their homes and their workplaces.

2. Once when she was traveling with Fred Mooney in Mexico, a crowd stopped the train and urged Mooney and she to open the train window.

3. Mooney and she were not sure whether they should open the window, but they decided to do so. When they did, she and him both were showered with red carnations and blue violets.

4. Although the people gave the flowers to both him and her, the flowers were meant as gifts in honor of "Madre Yones," as the people called her.

5. The trip to Mexico was exhausting, but it was she, over ninety years old, who never ran out of energy.

6. When Mooney fretted about her health, it was her who laughed and proposed that they get on with their sightseeing.

7. No one was more excited than her about the idea of a Pan-American Federation of Labor, an organization that would unite workers from Canada to South America.

8. The president of Mexico was as pleased as her at the idea of bringing together all the working people in the hemisphere.

9. "This is the beginning of a new day for us working people," exclaimed Mother Jones.

10. It was a day Mother Jones long remembered; years later it brought happy smiles to she and her friends whenever they saw carnations and violets or thought of that day's events.

Van Goor and Hacker, *Developmental Exercises for*
The Bedford Handbook, 9th ed. (Boston: Bedford, 2014)

24-2 | Pronoun and noun case   **77**

EXERCISE 24-3 ◆ Pronoun and noun case

To read about this topic, see section 24 in *The Bedford Handbook*, Ninth Edition.

Some of the personal pronouns in this passage are italicized; six of them are not in the correct case. The first one has been corrected for you. Find and correct the other five.

                   she

Though ~~her~~ and a friend would occasionally work together on the friend's campaign, Mother Jones avoided politics most of the time. *She*, the agitator, had no more interest in politics and political science than *her*, the labor organizer, had in economic theory. Mother Jones understood one kind of economics, the kind that dealt with wages, benefits, and the cost of bread and housing. The here-and-now problems of the poor called to Mother Jones so strongly that *she* had to do what *she* could to stop the injustice she saw around *her*.

Surprisingly, Mother Jones was not a supporter of woman suffrage. When the fight to win women's right to vote came along, it was not *her* who supported it. *Herself* and her people were the working classes, both men and women, and neither *she* nor *them* had much patience for the "society women" who led the movement. As far as Mother Jones was concerned, well-dressed women parading down the city streets carrying placards and banners did not help working men and women obtain a decent life. Mother Jones objected to *them* spending time and energy and money on activities that would not help her kind of people. Nor was *she* interested in helping a cause that would benefit only women; her concern was for all workers, regardless of gender. *She* seemed not to understand that the votes of the miners' wives might do as much to help the working men as *her* agitating and organizing did.

Van Goor and Hacker, *Developmental Exercises for The Bedford Handbook*, 9th ed. (Boston: Bedford, 2014)

EXERCISE 24-4 ◆ Pronoun and noun case: Guided review

Circle the correct pronoun or noun from each pair of words in parentheses. The numbers in the margin refer to relevant rules in section 24 of *The Bedford Handbook*, Ninth Edition. The first selection has been made for you.

Eventually, labor organizer Mother Jones began to think about her death. She wrote her autobiography and made plans for her burial, but she could not have dreamed how her name would be kept alive many years after her death.

(She / Her) and an editor friend began her autobiography when Mother Jones was ninety-two. Even with her friend working as hard as (she / her), Mother Jones found writing to be a grinding, demanding chore. Annoyed with her (friend / friend's) trying to make her remember details of her youth, she covered the first thirty years of her life in a few paragraphs. She had trouble remembering even the later years, confusing names and occasionally mixing up dates. She was never confused, however, about her conviction that working people were being unfairly treated. Nor did she doubt the necessity for (she / her) and her friends to help redress the wrongs done to working people.

24a

24d

24g

24f

Mother Jones planned to be buried in a place special to her. Back in 1898, four miners had been killed during a strike in Mount Olive, Illinois, and no cemetery in town would allow the bodies of these men to be buried on its land. So the union bought its own cemetery to bury them and others like them. For Mother Jones, burial in Miners Cemetery, Mount Olive, Illinois, was a way to say "(We / Us) working people have got to stick together" even after her death.

24e

She would have been puzzled by a memorial honoring her work. In the mid-twentieth century, a group of writers decided to publish a magazine devoted to exposing fraud and injustice in society. (They / Them) and their friends named this new publication *Mother Jones*. Mother Jones might not have appreciated the accolades it won or its citation by the *American Journalism Review* as "best in the business for investigative reporting," but she would have recognized at once the woman first listed under the journal's masthead: "Mother Jones (1830–1930)—Orator, Union Organizer, and Hellraiser."

24a

Van Goor and Hacker, *Developmental Exercises for The Bedford Handbook*, 9th ed. (Boston: Bedford, 2014)

24-4 | Pronoun and noun case: Guided review **79**

EXERCISE 25-1 ◆ *Who* and *whom*: Guided practice

Circle the correct pronoun from each pair in parentheses. The numbers in the margin refer to relevant rules in section 25 of *The Bedford Handbook*, Ninth Edition. The first selection has been made for you; answers to this exercise appear in the back of this book.

During World War II, American military officials were frustrated by Japanese

intelligence personnel, for (who /(whom)) deciphering American military codes was   25a

a relatively easy task. In response, Americans created codes that were increasingly

complex; however, the result was military leaders (who / whom) complained that   25a

deciphering new codes took hours. (Who / Whom) came to the rescue? It was a   25b

Californian by the name of Philip Johnston, (who / whom) had learned the Navajo   25a

language from the Navajos with (who / whom) his missionary family had grown up.   25a

Johnston was one of the few nonnatives (who / whom) was fluent in the complex   25a

Navajo language. Johnston knew that the Navajo language was extremely difficult to

learn and would be indecipherable to anyone (who / whom) was not associated with   25a

the Navajo people. The US Marines hired Johnston to develop a code talker program

using Navajo people.

Van Goor and Hacker, *Developmental Exercises for The Bedford Handbook*, 9th ed. (Boston: Bedford, 2014)

Name _____   Section _____   Date _____

EXERCISE 25-2 ◆ *Who* and *whom*

To read about this topic, see section 25 in *The Bedford Handbook*, Ninth Edition.

One sentence in each of the following pairs uses *who* and *whom* correctly and the other does not. Circle the letter next to the correct sentence. Example:

(a.) The US military intelligence recruited native Navajo speakers, whom the military referred to as wind talkers.

b. The US military intelligence recruited native Navajo speakers, who the military referred to as wind talkers.

1. **a.** In early 1942, Camp Pendleton, California, was home to a test unit of twenty-nine wind talkers, who were also known as code talkers.

   b. In early 1942, Camp Pendleton, California, was home to a test unit of twenty-nine wind talkers, whom were also known as code talkers.

2. **a.** The original group of code talkers consisted of enlistees of all ages, some of who were just young teenagers.

   b. The original group of code talkers consisted of enlistees of all ages, some of whom were just young teenagers.

3. **a.** The code talkers' assignment was to create a code based on the Navajo language that would be indecipherable to whoever was not a native Navajo speaker.

   b. The code talkers' assignment was to create a code based on the Navajo language that would be indecipherable to whomever was not a native Navajo speaker.

4. **a.** The code talkers, who had no Navajo words for "tank" or "dive-bombers," used their native words for "turtle" and "chicken hawk" instead.

   b. The code talkers, whom had no Navajo words for "tank" or "dive-bombers," used their native words for "turtle" and "chicken hawk" instead.

5. **a.** The military leaders who the code talkers were assigned to were impressed with the code talkers' keen abilities.

   b. The military leaders whom the code talkers were assigned to were impressed with the code talkers' keen abilities.

[*Note:* Sometimes the pronoun *whom* may be dropped without loss of clarity. Are there any *whom*s in the preceding sentences that you might choose to drop?]

Van Goor and Hacker, *Developmental Exercises for The Bedford Handbook*, 9th ed. (Boston: Bedford, 2014)

EXERCISE 25-3 ◆ *Who* and *whom*

To read about this topic, see section 25 in *The Bedford Handbook*, Ninth Edition.

Edit the following sentences to eliminate errors in the use of *who* and *whom*. Mark correct sentences "OK." Example:

> **The success of many World War II missions can be attributed to a small group of**
> *who*
> **Americans ~~whom~~ were known as code talkers.**
>   ^

1. Whom were these Americans? They were Native Americans from the Navajo nation.

2. Classified military information was transmitted by these Navajo code talkers, whom used a code based on their native language.

3. The Navajo code talkers, who were required to keep the code a secret, were not allowed to write down any of the words.

4. Anyone whom has studied American military history is aware of the significant role of the Navajo code talkers.

5. Everyone involved in the Marine landing in Iwo Jima knows whom to thank: the Navajo code talkers.

Van Goor and Hacker, *Developmental Exercises for The Bedford Handbook*, 9th ed. (Boston: Bedford, 2014)

EXERCISE 25-4 ◆ *Who* and *whom*: Guided review

Circle the correct pronoun from each pair in parentheses. The numbers in the margin refer to section 25 of *The Bedford Handbook*, Ninth Edition. The first selection has been made for you.

After World War II ended, the Navajo heroes (who / whom) served their country   25a

as code talkers returned home quietly, without recognition for their extraordinary

service. (Who / Whom) was responsible for this lack of acknowledgment to those   25b

(who / whom) America owed so much? It could not be helped. The US military   25c

considered the Navajo code so valuable that it was classified as a military secret

and later used in the Korean and Vietnam Wars. It wasn't until 1968 that the code

talker program was declassified, allowing (whoever / whomever) had participated in   25a

the missions to finally speak about the code talkers. It took many additional years

for the Navajo code talkers to receive national recognition for their unique service.

In 2001, they were honored by members of the Congress and President George W.

Bush, (who / whom) awarded the original twenty-nine code talkers the Congressional   25a

Gold Medal. This prestigious medal represents the deep admiration of and gratitude

to these Navajo code talkers, without (who / whom) many more American missions   25a

would have failed and many more American lives would have been lost. The code

talkers were further honored by John Woo, (who / whom) directed and helped produce   25a

Windtalkers, a 2002 fictionalized film of the code talkers' legendary mission.

Van Goor and Hacker, *Developmental Exercises for The Bedford Handbook*, 9th ed. (Boston: Bedford, 2014)

25-4 | *Who* and *whom*: Guided review   **83**

EXERCISE 26-1 ◆ Adjectives and adverbs: Guided practice

Edit the following paragraphs for correct use of adjectives and adverbs. The numbers in the margin refer to relevant rules in section 26 of *The Bedford Handbook*, Ninth Edition. The first revision has been done for you; answers to this exercise appear in the back of this book.

Novelists have often used their storytelling talents to influence people's

thinking. Charles Dickens did it in nineteenth-century England. From *David*

Copperfield to *Oliver Twist*, book after book depicted the plight of the poor and other

really

~~real~~ unfortunate members of society. Harriet Beecher Stowe did it in nineteenth-   26b

century America, but with not hardly as many books. Her *Uncle Tom's Cabin* depicted   26e

slavery so well that the book strongly influenced antislavery sentiments in the decade

before the Civil War.

Harriet Beecher Stowe considered slavery sinful and wanted her book to help

end slavery quick and peaceful. People first read parts of the novel ten years before the   26b

beginning of the war. An abolitionist magazine published the book a few chapters at a

time, hoping the effect of the story would make readers feel so badly about slavery that   26c

they would rally to the abolitionist cause. Many people, reading *Uncle Tom's Cabin*

installment by installment, did become convinced that nothing could be worser than   26d

living in slavery on a southern plantation.

None of the abolitionists, who devoted their energy to abolishing slavery,

expected a more perfect world when the book itself was published in 1852. But they   26d

certainly hoped that the book would be influential. It was. Of all the novels published

that year, it was the top seller on both sides of the Atlantic. Its popularity was good

news for the abolitionists. Harriet Beecher Stowe's wish had come true.

Van Goor and Hacker, *Developmental Exercises for
The Bedford Handbook*, 9th ed. (Boston: Bedford, 2014)

EXERCISE 26-2 ◆ Adjectives and adverbs

To read about this topic, see section 26 in *The Bedford Handbook*, Ninth Edition.

The two sentences in each of the following pairs are grammatically correct. The sentences have different meanings because one uses an adjective, the other an adverb. Read both sentences carefully to understand their meaning. Then circle the letter of the sentence that answers the question; be prepared to explain what the other sentence means. Example:

Which sentence means that southerners thought the book itself was dishonest?

a. Many southerners did not consider *Uncle Tom's Cabin* honest.

b. Many southerners did not consider *Uncle Tom's Cabin* honestly.

1. In which sentence did the people do a poor job of judging?

   a. Those people judged Mrs. Stowe's depiction of slave life inaccurate.

   b. Those people judged Mrs. Stowe's depiction of slave life inaccurately.

2. Which sentence says that the slaves had trouble finding the escape routes?

   a. Most slaves did not find their escape routes easy.

   b. Most slaves did not find their escape routes easily.

3. In which sentence do northerners think Stowe herself was honest?

   a. Most northerners believed Mrs. Stowe honest.

   b. Most northerners honestly believed Mrs. Stowe.

4. In which sentence did the judges think that some people had more rights than others?

   a. Southern judges did not consider all people equal.

   b. Southern judges did not consider all people equally.

5. Which sentence says that the overseers were looking scared?

   a. Rumors of escaping slaves made overseers look anxious when their slaves were out of sight.

   b. Rumors of escaping slaves made overseers look anxiously when their slaves were out of sight.

EXERCISE 26-3 ◆ Adjectives and adverbs

To read about this topic, see section 26 in *The Bedford Handbook*, Ninth Edition.

Six of the adjectives and adverbs in the following paragraphs are not used correctly. The first one has been corrected. Find and correct the other five.

Uncle Tom's Cabin was ~~real~~ *really* popular, even though it was a very long book. When it was published as a serial in the abolitionist magazine *National Era* in 1851 and 1852, people probably read all of it. But when the novel was published as a book, many people did not have enough time to read it. Since it had been a best-seller, enterprising publishers brought out new, abridged versions for more faster reading. By the end of the Civil War, many people knew the story of *Uncle Tom's Cabin* only from these shorter versions of it—both novels and plays.

Unfortunately, their knowledge was not only incomplete; it was distorted. Publishers left out important sections of this most priceless story. For example, in the book, Uncle Tom works for three different owners, two of whom treat him fairly good. But in the shortened versions of the story, Tom works for only one owner, who treats him very cruel. Even insensitive readers rightly found that cruel owner, Simon Legree, vicious and judged all slave owners by him. In addition, what had been a subplot in the novel—the story of George, Eliza, their baby, and the family's attempted escape to freedom in Canada—became a major portion of the story. Playwrights favored such dramatic subplots and incidents because they were easily dramatized.

Modern readers are often real surprised when they read the entire novel, a book that American critic Edmund Wilson called "a much more remarkable book than one had ever been allowed to suspect."

Van Goor and Hacker, *Developmental Exercises for The Bedford Handbook*, 9th ed. (Boston: Bedford, 2014)

EXERCISE 26-4 ◆ Adjectives and adverbs: Guided review

Edit the following paragraph for correct use of adjectives and adverbs. The numbers in the margin refer to relevant rules in section 26 of *The Bedford Handbook*, Ninth Edition. The first revision has been done for you.

Playwrights often find popular novels suitable for the stage. Produced as a

play, *Uncle Tom's Cabin* was the ~~successfulest~~ _∧ *most successful* stage play of the 1800s. The play used   26d

only the real dramatic portions of the novel and therefore somewhat slanted its basic   26b

message. Even worse than the plays were the "Tom Shows" that toured small towns

all over the North; these shows didn't contain scarcely anything but the violent scenes.   26e

Audiences felt very badly when they watched George and Eliza's desperate escape   26c

over the ice with their baby. Dramatists played on their viewers' sympathy with the

plight of this slave family. Viewers hoped until the very end that the family's escape

would work out perfect. Distortion was bad in both the plays and the Tom Shows, but   26b

it was worse in the Tom Shows, which turned this most unique story of slavery in the   26d

South into little more than propaganda. Particularly moving scenes from the story

continue to be used in plays and musicals. *The King and I* incorporated several. If a

modern movie is ever made from *Uncle Tom's Cabin*, the movie could very well reflect

the same distortions present in the old plays and the Tom Shows—and might be just

as popular.

Van Goor and Hacker, *Developmental Exercises for The Bedford Handbook*, 9th ed. (Boston: Bedford, 2014)

26-4 | Adjectives and adverbs: Guided review **87**

EXERCISE 27-1 ◆ Verb forms: Guided practice

Correct any nonstandard verb forms in the following paragraphs. The numbers in the margin refer to relevant rules in sections 27a to 27e of *The Bedford Handbook*, Ninth Edition. The first revision has been done for you; an answer to this exercise appears in the back of this book.

        Most Americans today ~~doesn't~~ *don't* realize that the American democratic system did   27c
not always include African Americans and women. The constitutional amendments
pass after the Civil War granted former slaves and all native-born African American   27d
men full voting rights, but the new amendments ignored women. Women had to wait
much longer—more than half a century—to be gave the right to vote.   27a

        Some individual states allowed women to vote as early as 1900, but by
1910 women activists decided to focus their energy on a federal amendment.
When Woodrow Wilson became president in 1913, women demonstrated along the
inauguration route, marching and holding signs demanding the vote for women. Then
in 1917, Alice Paul and a militant faction of the suffrage movement picketed the White
House and even chained themselves to fences. When the women were threaten and   27d
attacked by male mobs, police ignored the men and arrested the women. In prison,
the women endured filthy cells, force-feeding when they gone on a hunger strike, and   27a
ill treatment. Some women was restrained for many hours in uncomfortable positions   27a
with their arms high over their heads. One angry official repeatedly ask a doctor to   27d
declare one or more of the women insane. (The doctor refused.)

        President Wilson a man with major problems—a war abroad and women   27e
fighting for their rights at home. At first he tolerated the women picketers; he even
send coffee out to them. Then he just wanted the women to lie down their signs and   27a, 27b
banners and go home. But the increasing pressure from moderate and radical voices
in the movement as well as public outrage over the women's prison treatment finally
force Wilson to support a constitutional amendment for women's voting rights.   27d

Van Goor and Hacker, *Developmental Exercises for The Bedford Handbook,* 9th ed. (Boston: Bedford, 2014)

EXERCISE 27-2 ◆ Verb forms

To read about this topic, see sections 27a to 27e in *The Bedford Handbook*, Ninth Edition.

Edit the following paragraphs for missing *-ed* endings and incorrect forms of irregular verbs. The first revision has been done for you. You should make ten more.

            led
      Women who ~~leaded~~ the suffrage movement never used violence, but they thought of

themselves as waging a war. They tried different strategies in different places and coordinated

their various attacks. Some concentrated on state and local voting rights for women; others

work for national suffrage. In Washington, DC, they picketed, demonstrated, and builded and

maintained "perpetual watchfires" in which they burned the speeches on democracy that President

Wilson was giving in Europe.

      When the protesters were arrested at the White House in 1917, police had to use their

personal cars to carry the many prisoners they arrest. After the women and some of their

supporters were tried and found guilty, the judge got so tired of sentencing them that when he

reached twenty-six, he dismiss all the others.

      The women's organizing and demonstrating finally paid off. On May 21, 1919, the House of

Representatives passed the Nineteenth Amendment, giving women the right to vote, and sended it

to the Senate. On June 4, the Senate approved it and passed it along to the states for ratification.

      Women's groups kept up the pressure on the states during the long, tense ratification

process. When, after more than a year, thirty-five states had ratified the amendment, it all come

down to one man's vote in Tennessee. Whom do history remember as the hero of ratification? It was

a young legislator named Harry Burn, who cast the tie-breaking vote. On August 24, the governor

of Tennessee certified the vote and sent the results to Washington.

      The US secretary of state had tell his staff to wake him as soon as the certificate arrived.

He wanted to avoid a formal signing in the presence of the campaigning women. Nevertheless, on

August 26, 1920, more than seventy years after women had first began to organize for suffrage, it

was now official: Women in the United States had the right to vote.

Van Goor and Hacker, *Developmental Exercises for*
The Bedford Handbook, 9th ed. (Boston: Bedford, 2014)

27-2 | Verb forms **89**

EXERCISE 27-3 ◆ Verb forms

To read about this topic, see sections 27a to 27e in *The Bedford Handbook*, Ninth Edition.

Edit the following paragraphs to correct problems with *-s* and *-ed* verb forms. The first revision has been done for you. You should make ten more.

                         have
    Many historians ~~has~~ agreed that the woman suffrage movement in the United States is rooted in the Seneca Falls Convention of 1848. The convention was organize by Elizabeth Cady Stanton and Lucretia Mott, after Mott was denied a seat as a delegate at an antislavery convention in London.

    The Seneca Falls Convention is best known for a document produce by Stanton called the Declaration of Sentiments. Stanton's declaration remain one of the most important documents in American women's history. Modeled on the Declaration of Independence (1776), the Declaration of Sentiments list eighteen grievances—but these are grievances of women against their treatment by men and male-dominated society. Stanton's declaration explicitly state that "all men and women are created equal" and that women "demand the equal station to which they are entitled."

    A modern reader don't have to read more than a few sentences of each document to see the similarities between the two. In fact, it have been said that the Declaration of Sentiments might have been rejected if its format hadn't seemed so familiar to those who attended the convention. The Declaration of Independence demand that men in America, like men in England, be represented in government. The Declaration of Sentiments argue that women, like men, should be represented in government. The women's document go so far as to suggest that American women should have the right to vote. In 1848, this idea was shocking—so shocking that it would take seventy-two years for women's right to vote to become a reality.

Van Goor and Hacker, *Developmental Exercises for The Bedford Handbook*, 9th ed. (Boston: Bedford, 2014)

EXERCISE 27-4 ◆ Verb forms: Guided review

Correct any nonstandard verb use in the following paragraphs. The numbers in the margin refer to relevant rules in sections 27a to 27e of *The Bedford Handbook*, Ninth Edition. The first revision has been done for you.

                                                         doesn't

Today's American woman in a voting booth probably ~~don't~~ know how hard it was   **27c**

to win her the right to be there. It took thousands of women nearly a hundred years

to win that freedom for today's female voter. Many of those women who worked for

suffrage are no longer knowed, but their names should never be losted to history.   **27a, 27a**

    From the first organized call for woman suffrage in 1848 through the end of the

nineteenth century, feminists such as Elizabeth Cady Stanton, Lucretia Mott, Lucy

Stone, and Susan B. Anthony remained strong voices for women's rights. The next

generation of activists included Harriet Blatch, the youngest daughter of Stanton,

who carry on her mother's work, and Alice Blackwell, the daughter of Lucy Stone, who   **27d**

continued to edit the *Women's Journal*, which her mother had founded.

    In the early 1900s, the women took their cause to Washington. Just before

President Wilson's first inauguration in 1913, Inez Milholland, dressed in white and

riding a white horse, leaded eight thousand women in a march through Washington in   **27a**

support of the suffrage amendment. When she died at age thirty in 1916, a memorial

service was held for her in the US Capitol. She the first woman so honored.   **27e**

    Alice Paul devoted her life to suffrage, planning and executing demonstrations

and campaigns. Friends worried that she never laid down to rest but was always   **27b**

working for the cause. Paul's arrest and mistreatment in prison in 1918 were

instrumental in gaining President Wilson's support for the Nineteenth Amendment.

Lucy Burns got involved in woman suffrage in England, leaving her studies at Oxford

to work for the suffrage movement. When she come to the United States in 1913,   **27a**

she led others in civil disobedience and was arrested and jailed several times. Carrie

Chapman Catt develop the strategy for the final years of the battle. Her strategy was   **27d**

called "The Winning Plan," and eventually it become just that.   **27a**

    Today, most American women takes their right to vote for granted, unaware of   **27c**

the thousands of hands that opened the voting booth door for them.

Van Goor and Hacker, *Developmental Exercises for*
The Bedford Handbook, 9th ed. (Boston: Bedford, 2014)

27-4 | Verb forms: Guided review   **91**

EXERCISE 27-5 ◆ Verb tense and mood: Guided practice

Correct any tense or mood errors in the following paragraphs. The numbers in the margin refer to relevant rules in sections 27f and 27g of *The Bedford Handbook*, Ninth Edition. The first revision has been done for you; a suggested revision of this exercise appears in the back of this book.

Almost everyone has heard about Aesop's fables, but most people know very little about Aesop himself. Most of what we know about Aesop is a mixture of hearsay and conjecture. We do know that he was a slave in Greece. One theory is that before he came to Greece he *had* lived in Ethiopia for most of his life and that "Aesop" is a much-shortened form of "the Ethiopian."   27f

Aesop was not a storyteller then, though he would have loved to have spoken   27f well enough to tell a good story. He stuttered so badly that he did not even try to talk. In one story we learn, however, that he *could* communicate. A neighbor brought a gift of figs to Aesop's master. Greatly pleased, the master planned to enjoy the figs after his bath and directed that they were put in a cool place until he was ready. While   27g the master was bathing, the overseer and his friends ate the figs. When the master discovered the loss of his figs, the other slaves placed the blame on Aesop. They knew that if Aesop was able to speak, he could defend himself, but they did not fear this   27g stammering slave.

The master ordered that Aesop be flogged, but Aesop got the master to delay punishment briefly. After drinking a glass of warm water, Aesop ran his fingers down his throat and vomited only water. Pointing at the overseer, he made gestures that the overseer and his friends should do as he did. They drank the water, ran their fingers   27f down their throats — and vomited figs.

Although Aesop's cleverness saved him from a flogging, it also made an enemy of the overseer. Aesop discovered a basic truth about life: Being right didn't always help   27f one to make friends.

Van Goor and Hacker, *Developmental Exercises for The Bedford Handbook*, 9th ed. (Boston: Bedford, 2014)

EXERCISE 27-6 ◆ Verb tense and mood

To read about this topic, see sections 27f and 27g in *The Bedford Handbook*, Ninth Edition.

One sentence in each of the following pairs is correct; the other contains an error in tense or mood. Circle the letters of the correct sentences and edit the incorrect ones. Example:

(a.) **Aesop was sent to work in the farthest field because he had made an enemy of the overseer.**

b. **Maybe the overseer ~~hope~~ *hoped* Aesop would run away, or maybe he had forgotten that the field was next to a major road.**

1. a. One day a caravan that had lost its way came by the field where Aesop was working.

   b. The caravan driver requested that Aesop shows him the route to Cairo.

2. a. Aesop, who was unable to speak, wanted to have helped him, so he walked with the caravan until it was on the correct road.

   b. Grateful for Aesop's help and wanting to show his appreciation, the caravan leader offered Aesop a reward.

3. a. Aesop silently refused the reward; he had given his help without expecting anything in return.

   b. The caravan leader wanted to leave at once because he lost valuable time on his trip to Cairo.

4. a. When the caravan leader said good-bye, he asked the gods to bless Aesop.

   b. As the caravan moved out of sight, Aesop had decided to take a nap.

5. a. While Aesop slept, the gods restored his speech, proving that good deeds were sometimes rewarded.

   b. When Aesop awoke and could speak, he rejoiced that the gods help those who befriend strangers.

Van Goor and Hacker, *Developmental Exercises for*
The Bedford Handbook, 9th ed. (Boston: Bedford, 2014)

27-6 | Verb tense and mood   **93**

EXERCISE 27-7 ◆ Verb tense and mood

To read about this topic, see sections 27f and 27g in *The Bedford Handbook*, Ninth Edition.

Some of the italicized verbs in the following sentences are correct; others are in the wrong mood. Mark the correct sentences "OK," and change any incorrect verbs. Example:

> **In ancient Greek culture, an overseer usually tried to sell a troublesome slave; if the slave**
>
> ***was* sold, the overseer's life would be easier.**   *OK*

1. When his Greek slave owner ordered that Aesop *be* sold, it was hard to find a buyer for him because he was so ugly.

2. Finally Aesop requested that he *be* allowed to sell himself.

3. Aesop knew that if he *was* not so ugly, many buyers would be glad to get him.

4. If he *was* going to find a buyer, Aesop would need to be clever.

5. One day a caravan that *was* in the slave-trading business stopped at Aesop's master's house.

6. The caravan driver requested that the slave owner *sells* him at least one strong slave.

7. The driver saw that Aesop's muscles *were* strong, but Aesop's hunched back and ugly face discouraged him.

8. Aesop realized that his chances of getting away *were* slim.

9. "If I *was* handsome, I would not be useful as a bogeyman to scare any misbehaving children," he said.

10. If he *were* afraid, the caravan owner did not show it; he laughed at Aesop—and bought him.

Van Goor and Hacker, *Developmental Exercises for The Bedford Handbook*, 9th ed. (Boston: Bedford, 2014)

EXERCISE 27-8 ◆ Verb tense and mood: Guided review

Correct any errors in verb tense or mood in the following paragraphs. The numbers in the margin refer to relevant rules in sections 27f and 27g of *The Bedford Handbook*, Ninth Edition. The first revision has been done for you. You should make five more.

Aesop's death illustrated the implied moral of his last fable: When two enemies

fight each other, it ~~was~~ *is* wise to watch for a larger enemy of both. Aesop's death came   27f

some years after one of his owners gave him his freedom. His former owner would   27f

have liked Aesop to have stayed in the same town, but Aesop became an adviser at the   27f

courts of several kings.

One of those kings, Croessus, sent Aesop to Delphi to distribute some gifts. The

people of Delphi demanded that he gives them the gifts at once. Aesop refused, having   27g

discovered that the people of Delphi had lied to Croessus about their activities. The

angry people decided that if Aesop was dead, they could distribute the gifts as they   27g

pleased. These people threw Aesop over a cliff to his death, but not before Aesop had

told one more story.

In the story, a frog invites a rat to dinner. To help the rat across the river to the

frog's house, the frog ties one of the rat's legs to one of his own. Midstream, the frog

tries to drown the rat. The rat puts up such a fight that an eagle flying overhead sees

the commotion and promptly eats both of them.

"You will succeed in killing me," said Aesop to the people of Delphi, "but a larger

enemy will kill you as well." After Aesop's death, terrible plagues devastated the city.

People believed that the plagues came because of what they did to Aesop. To this day,   27f

the expression "blood of Aesop" refers to an innocent person whose death someone has

avenged.

Van Goor and Hacker, *Developmental Exercises for*
The Bedford Handbook, 9th ed. (Boston: Bedford, 2014)

27-8 | Verb tense and mood: Guided review   **95**

REVIEW OF 19–27 ◆ Grammatical sentences

Edit the following paragraphs to eliminate grammatical errors. The numbers in the margin refer to relevant rules in sections 19–27 of *The Bedford Handbook*, Ninth Edition. First try to find and correct the errors on your own. Then look up the rules if you need to. The first revision has been done for you.

represent The fables of Aesop ~~represents~~ the Western root of fable, but there are two	21a

strong Eastern roots of fable also: the Panchatantra and the Jataka tales.

The Panchatantra is a collection of stories designed to teach a first prince and	
his brothers how to rule over a kingdom. (Until a tutor taught the first prince with	
these stories, him and his brothers would never stay in the schoolroom. The boys	24a
listened eagerly to this new tutor who their father had found.) They are usually longer	25a, 23a
than Western fables and have people as well as animals for characters. Their tone	
sounds differently, too. Aesop's fables make gentle fun of people's foibles, Panchatantra	26a, 20b
fables teach lessons in how to achieve and hold power. This difference is easily	
recognize in the moral to one of the Panchatantra fables: "Do not strike an enemy of	27d
iron with a fist of flesh. Wait until your enemy is stranded at the bottom of a well.	
Then throw stones upon him."	

The stories that carry the name Jataka tells about the Buddha and the	21a
adventures he had when he came to earth in various incarnations. In these stories, the	
Buddha appeared as an animal. Or sometimes simply as a "wise old man." Like the	27f, 19b
Aesop stories, the Jataka tales often depict people's foibles and shortcomings, but the	
Jataka tales are not satiric. And they promote compassion rather than power. In one	
story, for example, monkeys try to help their friend the gardener by watering newly	
planted trees for him. In doing so, they pull each tree out of the ground to see how	
long their roots are. Of course the trees die. The Buddha comments, "The ignorant and	22a
foolish, even when they desire to do good, often do ill."	

      Putting all three traditions of fable together, any reader can choose from a rich

combination of small stories that carry large messages.

Van Goor and Hacker, *Developmental Exercises for The Bedford Handbook,* 9th ed. (Boston: Bedford, 2014)

EXERCISE 28-1 ◆ ESL verb use: Guided practice

Edit the following paragraphs to correct problems with verbs. The numbers in the margin refer to relevant rules in section 28 of *The Bedford Handbook*, Ninth Edition. You may need to refer to the list in 27a for the correct form for some irregular verbs. The first revision has been done for you; a suggested revision of this exercise appears in the back of this book.

                      come

     Immigrants have ~~came~~ to the United States from all over the world. Initially,   28a

new settlers were mostly European, Irish, or English. By the early twentieth century,

many Asians had took a frightening boat trip across the Pacific to get here. Usually   28a

the men came first. After they had made enough money for passage, their wives and

children were bring over. All thought that if they worked hard, they will make a   28b, 28e

good life, as earlier European immigrants had done. A large number of Chinese and

Japanese settled in the western part of the United States.

     These new immigrants worked on the railroads and in the mines. American

businesses recruited Chinese labor because American workers would not accepted   28c

the wages that were paying. Why did workers decide to come to America anyway?   28b

Somehow the idea got started that America was a "golden mountain" where people

could picked up gold nuggets after an easy climb. Once they got here, most immigrants   28c

worked hard because they hoped making enough money to bring relatives to America   28f

too.

     Before and during World War II, many Germans who had been persecuted

by Hitler escaped to America. After the war, thousands of "displaced persons" were

welcome by the United States. Later, refugees from Asia, Africa, Latin America, and   28b

the Caribbean wanted being accepted. Franklin D. Roosevelt once said, "All of our   28f

people all over the country, except the pure-blooded Indians, are immigrants or

descendants of immigrants." If Roosevelt were alive today, he will know that his   28e

statement is still true.

EXERCISE 28-2 ◆ Verb forms

To read about this topic, see section 28a in *The Bedford Handbook*, Ninth Edition.

Use the tense indicated at the end of each sentence to write the correct form of the verb in brackets. Example:

People from many countries ___*entered*___ [*enter*] the United States in the 1980s. [Past]

1. Eighty percent of the immigrants who _____ [*migrate*] to the United States in the 1980s were Asian or Latin American. [Past]

2. The number of Asians who _____ [*live*] in the United States more than doubled between 1970 and 1980. [Past progressive]

3. People from the Philippines, China, and Korea _____ [*be*] regular immigrants to the United States. [Present perfect]

4. Since 1975, a rush of immigrant refugees _____ [*arrive*] in the United States. [Present perfect progressive]

5. In less than a seven-year period, 600,000 refugees from Vietnam, Laos, and Cambodia _____ [*come*] to the United States. [Past]

Van Goor and Hacker, *Developmental Exercises for The Bedford Handbook*, 9th ed. (Boston: Bedford, 2014)

EXERCISE 28-3 ◆ Helping verbs, main verbs, and omitted verbs

To read about this topic, see sections 28a to 28d in *The Bedford Handbook*, Ninth Edition.

A | In the following sentences, underline the correct phrase in parentheses. Example:

Jacqueline Cochran's life story (<u>has captured</u> / has capture) the interest of World War II and aircraft historians.

1. Jacqueline Cochran (grow / grew) up in rural northwest Florida in the early 1900s.

2. As a young girl, she (was employed / was employ) as a shampoo girl for a hairdresser.

3. Since she liked the work, she decided that she (would go / would gone) to New York City to start her own line of cosmetics.

4. In 1932, she met her future husband, Floyd Bostwick Odlum, who suggested that she (should get / should to get) a pilot's license to promote her business.

5. Jacqueline Cochran later claimed that the flying lessons (had change / had changed) her life.

B | Edit the following sentences for incorrect use of verbs. Put "OK" next to the one correct sentence. Example:

                          want
Jacqueline Cochran did not ~~wanted~~ to stop with basic flying lessons.

6. In 1934, she compete in air races.

7. By 1937, several air speed and altitude records were hold by Jacqueline Cochran.

8. After World War II began, she traveled to Europe to investigate how female pilots could help the war effort.

9. In 1942, Jacqueline Cochran ask General Henry "Hap" Arnold to create an American organization of women pilots.

10. This organization would eventually be know as the Women Airforce Service Pilots.

Van Goor and Hacker, *Developmental Exercises for The Bedford Handbook*, 9th ed. (Boston: Bedford, 2014)

28-3 | Helping verbs, main verbs, and omitted verbs **99**

EXERCISE 28-4 ◆ Verb forms

To read about this topic, see sections 28a to 28d in *The Bedford Handbook*, Ninth Edition.

Turn each of the following sentence openings into a complete sentence using the correct form of one of the following: *give, name, take, buy, offer.* Example:

I did not *offer to make coffee.* _____

1. They had been _____

2. He could not _____

3. An award was _____

4. She has already _____

5. They must _____

6. Immigrants have _____

7. Your father has not _____

8. My uncle could _____

9. The house is _____

10. I have been _____

Van Goor and Hacker, *Developmental Exercises for*
The Bedford Handbook, 9th ed. (Boston: Bedford, 2014)

EXERCISE 28-5 ◆ Passive verbs

To read about this topic, see section 28b in *The Bedford Handbook*, Ninth Edition.

Edit the italicized verb or verb phrase in each of the following sentences to correct the error in the use of helping verbs or main verbs. The revised verbs should all be in the passive voice. You may need to refer to the list in 27a for the correct form of some irregular verbs. Example:

> In the early twentieth century, so many immigrants wanted to enter the United States that
> a special center *was* ~~*build*~~ to process them.
>   built

1. That center, Ellis Island, *had constructed* to handle five thousand people a day, but often ten thousand people were processed in one day.

2. All immigrants *were check* by a doctor, and an immigrant's coat was marked with a code if the doctor suspected a problem.

3. Everyone knew that if an immigrant *was gave* an "X," the immigrant had practically no chance to enter America; an "X" meant "possible mental problems."

4. Sometimes families were divided because one child was rejected for some reason; often the child *would sent* back alone.

5. Although it was the entrance to a new life for many people, "Ellis Island" *was translate* as "Isle of Tears" in many European languages.

Van Goor and Hacker, *Developmental Exercises for The Bedford Handbook,* 9th ed. (Boston: Bedford, 2014)

28-5 | Passive verbs   **101**

EXERCISE 28-6 ◆ Conditional verbs

To read about this topic, see section 28e in *The Bedford Handbook*, Ninth Edition.

Edit the following paragraph to correct problems with conditional verbs. You may need to refer to the list in 27a for the correct form of some irregular verbs. The first revision has been done for you. You should make five more.

      If my great-grandfather had immigrated today, instead of one hundred years ago, he

probably ~~will~~ *would* have traveled by jet. He came from Croatia to the United States just before the First

World War. In those days, when people left their native country, they usually do so forever. My

great-grandfather missed Croatia, but he liked America very much. He always said that America

was a country where if you work hard, you would be successful. My great-grandfather, who will

be 115 years old if he were alive today, was not as successful as he had hoped. If he has earned

more money, he would have gone back to Croatia to visit. I'm sure my great-grandfather will have

enjoyed that trip if he had ever had the chance to make it.

Van Goor and Hacker, *Developmental Exercises for The Bedford Handbook*, 9th ed. (Boston: Bedford, 2014)

EXERCISE 28-7 ◆ Verbs followed by gerunds or infinitives

To read about this topic, see section 28f in *The Bedford Handbook*, Ninth Edition.

The gerunds and infinitives are italicized in the following sentences. Only one in each sentence is correct; correct the other one. Example:

> In 1943, under the leadership of Jacqueline Cochran, women pilots who wanted *serving* ^to serve^ their country during World War II began *arriving* at Avenger Field in Sweetwater, Texas, for training.

1. About 25,000 women wanted *being* accepted into the Women Airforce Service Pilots (WASP) program, but only 1,830 applicants were accepted, and only 1,074 managed *to complete* the challenging flight training.

2. The WASP trainees learned *to fly* aircraft such as the Fairchild PT-19 and the North American AT-6; they appreciated *to have* this rare opportunity to fly powerful military aircraft.

3. Following graduation, some female pilots were assigned *to deliver* aircraft from air base to air base or from factories to air bases. Others became test pilots or were assigned *flying* practice targets behind their planes for male pilot trainees to shoot at.

4. Some male pilots back then resented *sharing* their distinctive status as military pilots with women, but most of the women recalled *to be* treated with acceptance and respect.

5. As World War II was beginning *winding* down, the WASP program was disbanded. Many disappointed female pilots offered to keep *flying* for a dollar a year; however, their offer was declined, and the WASP organization officially ended in December 1944.

Van Goor and Hacker, *Developmental Exercises for The Bedford Handbook*, 9th ed. (Boston: Bedford, 2014)

28-7 | Verbs followed by gerunds or infinitives **103**

EXERCISE 28-8 ◆ Verbs followed by gerunds or infinitives

To read about this topic, see section 28f in *The Bedford Handbook*, Ninth Edition.

Correct the use of gerunds and infinitives in the following sentences. Put "OK" next to the one correct sentence. Example:

> The members of the Women Airforce Service Pilots (WASP) never considered ~~to quit~~ *quitting* despite the risks.

1. While the WASP pilots were well qualified and well trained, they were often required *flying* brand-new aircraft or aircraft with mechanical problems.

2. Official WASP records report *to lose* thirty-eight women in aircraft accidents.

3. Since the female pilots were technically civil service, not military, the military refused *to pay* burial expenses for any who were killed during their service.

4. When one of these brave women died, her fellow pilots donated money and volunteered *accompanying* the body home to her family.

5. The WASP families were not allowed *draping* an American flag over the casket during the funeral, but many families did so anyway.

Van Goor and Hacker, *Developmental Exercises for The Bedford Handbook*, 9th ed. (Boston: Bedford, 2014)

EXERCISE 28-9 ◆ ESL verb use: Guided review

Edit the following paragraphs to correct errors in the use of verbs. The numbers in the margin refer to relevant rules in section 28 of *The Bedford Handbook*, Ninth Edition. The first sentence has been revised for you.

 During World War II, the Women Airforce Service Pilots (WASP) ~~train~~ *trained* with   28b
male military recruits, yet they were considered civil service. Uniforms were not
provide, so while they flew, the women wore "zoot suits," ill-fitting coveralls designed   28b
for male pilots. The female pilots no allowed into the military officers' clubs. If a   28c
woman was kill in the line of duty, other female pilots donated money to send the body   28e
home. After the WASP organization was deactivated in December 1944, each woman
had to pay her own way home. Because they did not have military status, the women
were not allowed receiving veterans' benefits until 1977.   28f

 Finally, thanks to the efforts of sympathetic senators and representatives,
Congress decided awarding the Women Airforce Service Pilots the highest civilian   28f
honor: the Congressional Gold Medal. In March 2010, about two hundred surviving
WASP members traveled to Washington, DC, with their families to accept this long
overdue recognition for their service.

 The story of the Women Airforce Service Pilots has been miss from aviation   28a
history chapters until now. Now, these women are recognize as true aviation pioneers.   28c
They opened the door for other women to served in the armed forces as pilots and   28a
become astronauts. Air Force Lieutenant Colonel Nicole Malachowski, who was the
first female pilot for the Air Force's Thunderbirds, a precision air demonstration
squadron, also work on the bill for the Congressional Gold Medal and spoke at the   28a
ceremony. "Their motives for wanting to flying airplanes all those years ago weren't   28f
for fame or glory or recognition. They simply had a passion to take what gifts they
had and use them to help defend not only America, but the entire free world, from
tyranny," Lt. Col. Malachowski said.

Van Goor and Hacker, *Developmental Exercises for*
The Bedford Handbook, 9th ed. (Boston: Bedford, 2014)

28-9 | ESL verb use: Guided review   **105**

EXERCISE 29-1 ◆ Articles: Guided practice

Edit the following paragraphs to correct the use of articles. The numbers in the margin refer to relevant rules in section 29 of *The Bedford Handbook*, Ninth Edition. The first revision has been done for you; a suggested revision of this exercise appears in the back of this book.

People all over the world have stories that are part of their culture. Many

cultures have ^*a* creation story that explains how the world came to be. Sometimes   29c

story tells how a single piece of the world got its characteristics. It is not surprising   29b

that these stories exist; what is surprising is how similar the stories are. Consider

Cinderella story, for example. Cinderella has different names in different places,   29b

and details of her adventure are not the same; but the basic story echoes around a   29b

world.

In the Egypt, she is called Rhodopis (the word means "rosy cheeked"). Rhodopis   29f

is a Greek slave in a Egyptian home. She does not have eyes or an hair like anyone   29a, 29d

else in the home. Her green eyes look quite different from eyes of the other girls. Their   29b

dark, straight hair almost never gets tangled; her yellow, curly hair blows into tangled   29c

mass around her face. Her light-skinned face turns red and burns when she is in sun   29b

too long. When someone calls her "Rosy Rhodopis," she blushes, and her cheeks become

rosier.

Unable to make the friends with the other girls, Rhodopis turns to the animals   29e

in the nearby woods and streams for companionship.

Van Goor and Hacker, *Developmental Exercises for The Bedford Handbook*, 9th ed. (Boston: Bedford, 2014)

EXERCISE 29-2 ◆ Articles

To read about this topic, see section 29 in *The Bedford Handbook*, Ninth Edition.

Some of the following sentences contain errors in the use of articles. Mark the correct sentences "OK" and correct the others. Example:

> Rhodopis charmed the animals: birds, monkeys, and even ~~an~~ *a* hippopotamus would do what she asked.

1. The animals loved to watch her dance; her tiny feet seemed never to touch path.

2. One night when her owner saw her dancing, he was enchanted and decided that such feet deserved special shoes.

3. Rhodopis's shoes had the leather soles, but the toes had a gold on them.

4. When Rhodopis danced, shoes sparkled; they seemed alive.

5. Jealous, the servant girls gave her the more chores; by nighttime, Rhodopis was almost too tired for a single dance.

6. Pharaoh, the ruler of Egypt, sent out a invitation for all his subjects to appear at a court festival.

7. Everyone wanted to go to festival; Rhodopis looked forward to dancing there.

8. The other girls gave her extra chores so that she would not be able to get away: washing the clothes, grinding the grain, and planting the garden.

9. While Rhodopis was doing a laundry, a hippopotamus splashed into the water.

10. The splash muddied Rhodopis's shoes; she cleaned the shoes and set them high on the riverbank to keep them safe.

Van Goor and Hacker, *Developmental Exercises for The Bedford Handbook*, 9th ed. (Boston: Bedford, 2014)

29-2 | Articles **107**

EXERCISE 29-3 ◆ Articles

To read about this topic, see section 29 in *The Bedford Handbook*, Ninth Edition.

Some of the following sentences are missing one article or contain a misused article. Mark the correct sentences "OK" and correct the others. Example:

> Almost as soon as Rhodopis put her slippers on the bank, ^*a*^ huge shadow fell over the land.

1. Rhodopis looked up and saw an huge falcon flying overhead.

2. Rhodopis bowed her head, recognizing the falcon as a symbol of great god Horus.

3. She greeted the bird politely; but when bird flew away, he took one of her slippers with him.

4. Tearful, Rhodopis tucked the other slipper into her tunic and resumed a work.

5. She tried to imagine dancing on one foot; idea made her laugh.

6. The bird flew to Memphis, went to the festival, and found the pharaoh, Amasis.

7. Amasis sat on his throne, immobilized by a boredom; then the bird dropped the shoe into his lap.

8. Amasis recognized Horus in the falcon and decided that the shoe was a sign to tell him whom he should marry.

9. Amasis got into his chariot to look all through Egypt for owner of the shoe, who he knew would be his bride.

10. All of people went home from the festival, including the servant girls who had left Rhodopis at home.

Van Goor and Hacker, *Developmental Exercises for The Bedford Handbook*, 9th ed. (Boston: Bedford, 2014)

	ISBN	Qty	Sales Order
	9781457650789	1	F 17941803 1

Customer P/O No
P0034323
Title: Developmental Exercises for the Bedford Handbook

Format:	P (Paperback)
Author:	Hacker, Diana ; Sommers, Nancy
Publisher:	Bedford Books
Fund:	120
Location:	HUMN – BK
Loan Type:	1409A00
Coutts CN:	25722447

Order Specific Instructions

JT 1409A00 F

Ship To:
HUMBER COLLEGE INSTITUTE
P0034323
C/O OCLC CANADA
LIBRARY TECHNICAL SERVICE
1465 ST. JAMES STREET
WINNIPEG MB R3H 0W9

Volume:	
Edition:	0009
Year:	2013
Pagination:	208 p.
Size:	28 x 22 cm

Routing   1
SORTING
F02B01X
Shipping

34393932 USFWLG16 RC2

EXERCISE 29-4 ◆ Articles: Guided review

Edit the following paragraphs to correct the use of articles. The numbers in the margin refer to relevant rules in section 29 of *The Bedford Handbook*, Ninth Edition. The first revision has been done for you.

Pharaoh Amasis traveled all over ~~the~~ Egypt searching for his bride-to-be. The   29f

search took the very long time. Everywhere, beautiful women came to put their feet   29c

into a rose-gold slipper he carried with him. Not one of them could fit her foot into so   29b

small a shoe.

When Amasis had not found the owner of the shoe in his own land, he decided

to look along Nile River. His boats were brightly decorated, and musicians made an   29f, 29a

loud noise of trumpets and gongs as they traveled. The noise attracted many people

to river, but Rhodopis was so frightened that she ran to hide in a weed patch. Amasis   29b

stopped his boat so that the people along the shore could reach him and pay an   29d

attention to his words.

When Amasis held out the slipper, all of the servant girls made effort to put it   29c

on; it fit no one. Then Amasis saw Rhodopis in weeds and ordered her to try it on also.   29b

The shoe fit, and Rhodopis pulled its mate out of her tunic.

Wearing both slippers, Rhodopis joined Amasis on a boat. Rhodopis was on her   29b

way to an happy life as the new queen of Egypt.   29a

EXERCISE 30/31-1 ◆ Sentence structure, prepositions, and idiomatic expressions: Guided practice

Edit the following paragraphs to correct any misuses of subjects, repetitions, adverbs, adjectives, participles, and prepositions. The numbers in the margin refer to relevant rules in sections 30 and 31 of *The Bedford Handbook*, Ninth Edition. The first revision has been done for you; a suggested revision of this exercise appears in the back of this book.

A descendant of one of the earliest immigrants ~~at~~ *to* North America played a   31a

pivotal role in helping later Americans explore their country. Were tribes of American   30b

Indians living all over what is now the United States. Each tribe had its own language

and customs. Some tribes raided others and took prisoners who then became the

raiding tribes' slaves. That is what happened to a young Shoshone girl now known as

Sacagawea.

This girl, like many young girls, she had a nickname, "He-toe." "He-toe" was the   30c

sound a local bird made, and the girl's movements were as swift as that bird's. When a

raiding party of Hidatsas captured easily this young girl, they named her Sacagawea —   30f

"bird woman." Sacagawea was about twelve years old. The frightening young girl did   30g

not try to escape but accepted her role and worked for her captors. At a few months,   31a

she had acquired a reputation for good sense and good work.

The tribe married Sacagawea to a white man, Toussaint Charbonneau; she was

his second wife. Soon pregnant, this typical Indian wife she did the chores and left all   30c

decisions to her husband; but inwardly, she longed to explore new places and meet new

people. She may have been controlling by her husband, but she never missed a chance   30g

to learn whatever she could.

When white men appeared, many Indians were curious. Sacagawea had never

seen a man with yellow hair — or red hair. Nor had she ever seen a black man. All

these men were trying to get to the "Big Water" far to the west. They would have to

cross mountains that they had not even seen them yet. They needed horses and guides   30d

that the Shoshone could supply and an interpreter who could speak the Shoshone

language. Imagine their surprise when this interpreter, whom they had hoped to find

him, turned out to be a woman — a Shoshone young attractive woman.   30d, 30h

Van Goor and Hacker, *Developmental Exercises for The Bedford Handbook*, 9th ed. (Boston: Bedford, 2014)

EXERCISE 30/31-2 ◆ Omissions and needless repetitions

To read about this topic, see sections 30b to 30d in *The Bedford Handbook*, Ninth Edition.

In the following sentences, add needed subjects or expletives and delete any repeated subjects, objects, or adverbs. Mark the two correct sentences "OK." Example:

> **The white men who came ashore ~~they~~ had been sent by the Great White Father in**
>
> **Washington to blaze a trail to the Big Water.**

1. The two leaders among the white men they were Meriwether Lewis and William Clark.

2. Clark's red beard and hair puzzled Sacagawea; was hard to believe that those red hairs were real.

3. Sacagawea also watched in amazement as York, the black man, he washed his hands and face and none of his color came off.

4. The men quickly began building the shelters that they were going to live in them.

5. Was a lot of noise as they felled trees and fitted the logs together to build cabins.

6. The white men hired Charbonneau as an interpreter (he spoke both Hidatsa and French) and told him to bring Sacagawea along too.

7. Sacagawea could hardly believe that she would see her own people again in the place where she had lived there before.

8. Charbonneau and Sacagawea, who was now near the end of her pregnancy, were given a cabin to live in that winter.

9. Sacagawea's friends came often to the house that she was staying in it, usually asking for medical help while they were there.

10. Sacagawea, who learned how to cook for the white men, she tried especially to please Captain Clark, who gave her an English name, Janie.

Van Goor and Hacker, *Developmental Exercises for The Bedford Handbook,* 9th ed. (Boston: Bedford, 2014)

30/31-2 | Omissions and needless repetitions   **111**

EXERCISE 30/31-3 ◆ Present and past participles

To read about this topic, see section 30g in *The Bedford Handbook*, Ninth Edition.

Circle the letter of the sentence that answers the question. Example:

In which sentence were the men eager to get started?

a. **By April, the snows were melting and the men in the camp were exciting to begin moving on.**

(b.) **By April, the snows were melting and the men in the camp were excited to begin moving on.**

1. In which sentence were the men happy?

   a. Sacagawea always found the men pleasing.

   b. Sacagawea always found the men pleased.

2. In which sentence was Sacagawea eager to get to the mountains?

   a. As they neared the mountains, where the Shoshone lived, Sacagawea grew more and more excited.

   b. As they neared the mountains, where the Shoshone lived, Sacagawea grew more and more exciting.

3. In which sentence did Clark enjoy watching Sacagawea?

   a. Watching Sacagawea bargain for horses, Clark was fascinating.

   b. Watching Sacagawea bargain for horses, Clark was fascinated.

4. In which sentence were the travelers unhappy?

   a. For the four months they stayed on the West Coast, the travelers had only twelve days without rain; all of them found this weather depressed.

   b. For the four months they stayed on the West Coast, the travelers had only twelve days without rain; all of them found this weather depressing.

5. In which sentence did the decision make everyone fearful?

   a. On the way home, Lewis and Clark made a frightened decision to divide the crew and send the men along different trails.

   b. On the way home, Lewis and Clark made a frightening decision to divide the crew and send the men along different trails.

Van Goor and Hacker, *Developmental Exercises for The Bedford Handbook*, 9th ed. (Boston: Bedford, 2014)

EXERCISE 30/31-4 ◆ Placement of adjectives

To read about this topic, see section 30h in *The Bedford Handbook*, Ninth Edition.

Insert the given adjectives in their correct positions in the following sentences. Do not add commas. Example:

> **old, experienced**
>
> <u>Experienced</u> _____<u>old</u>_____ **women came to help Sacagawea when it was time for her baby to be born.**

1. log, warm

   Sacagawea was glad that she was living in a _____ _____ cabin when birthing

   time came.

2. hard, labor

   The baby did not come easily. Neither the old women's skill nor Captain Clark's medicines

   did much to ease Sacagawea's _____ _____ pains.

3. the, old, bell-shaped

   Finally, one of the men said that swallowing some rattles (_____ _____

   _____ scales on a rattlesnake's tail) often brought a quick and easy birth.

4. dark, strange, this

   Captain Clark had collected some rattles; he crushed two of them and added some water.

   One of the old women gave _____ _____ _____ potion to Sacagawea.

5. male, a, healthy

   Ten minutes later, Jean Baptiste Charbonneau arrived—_____ _____

   _____ child who would be affectionately called "Pomp," the Shoshone word for

   "firstborn."

Van Goor and Hacker, *Developmental Exercises for*
The Bedford Handbook, 9th ed. (Boston: Bedford, 2014)

30/31-4 | Placement of adjectives   113

EXERCISE 30/31-5 ◆ Sentence structure, prepositions, and idiomatic expressions: Guided review

Edit the following paragraphs to correct any misuses of subjects, repetitions, adverbs, adjectives, participles, and prepositions. Do not change correct sentences. The numbers in the margin refer to relevant rules in sections 30 and 31 of *The Bedford Handbook*, Ninth Edition. The first revision has been done for you.

By the time Lewis and Clark ̸found ̸ finally ̸ the Pacific Ocean and made their way   30f

home again, Sacagawea not only had gotten her wish to travel but also had become a

favorite of all the crew. Had served as interpreter, guide, cook, nurse, and mother for   30b

everyone who needed her. She and Pomp seemed like family to Clark and his men.

When Captain Clark left, he offered to take Pomp (now almost two) to St.

Louis and educate him. Sacagawea said, "Not now," but later the whole family moved

in St. Louis. No one is sure what happened next. Most historians agree that after   31a

a few months Charbonneau left gladly St. Louis "with his wife" and spent time at   30f

a new fort, Fort Manuel. There his wife she sickened and died of a fever in 1812.   30c

Since Charbonneau had several Shoshone wives, cannot be sure that this wife was   30b

Sacagawea. Historical records show that Clark became the legal guardian for Pomp

and his baby sister the year that Charbonneau's wife died.

Pomp stayed with Captain Clark. At nineteen, he met a German rich prince who   30h

was touring America and went to Europe with him for six years. Later this mountain

man, whose mother had trekked with him halfway across the continent before he

could walk, he returned to mountain life for good, working as a trader, a hunter, and   30c

an interpreter.

The Shoshone oral tradition says that Sacagawea quarreled with Charbonneau

and left him, stayed for a while with the Comanches, met up with her son and a

nephew, and ended up at the Wind River Reservation in Wyoming, where she died on

April 4, 1884, almost one hundred years old. The Wyoming branch of the Daughters of

the American Revolution were convincing that the oral tradition was true and erected   30g

a memorial stone there.

Van Goor and Hacker, *Developmental Exercises for*
The Bedford Handbook, 9th ed. (Boston: Bedford, 2014)

30/31-5 | Sentence structure, prepositions, and idiomatic
expressions: Guided review   **115**

No other American woman has had so many memorials dedicated to her. Among them are historical markers, lakes, a river, a mountain peak, and a park. On 1999, the United States even honored her on its new dollar—a gold-colored coin. Just below the word *Liberty* on that coin is a likeness of Sacagawea with her infant son. Now travel-loving Sacagawea can go wherever that dollar goes there.

31a

30d

Van Goor and Hacker, *Developmental Exercises for The Bedford Handbook,* 9th ed. (Boston: Bedford, 2014)

REVIEW OF 28–31 ◆ Multilingual writers and ESL challenges

This paragraph has eleven errors. The numbers in the margin refer to relevant rules in sections 28–31 of *The Bedford Handbook*, Ninth Edition. You may need to refer to the list in 27a for the correct form of some irregular verbs. The first revision has been done for you. Find and correct ten more errors.

Immigrants have ~~gave~~ *given* the United States their languages, their foods, and	28a
their customs. Many people are not aware for all the cultural influences. Native	31c
Americans gave the United States the names for half of its states. *Texas* is a	
Native American old word for "friends," and *Idaho* means "good morning." Spanish	30h
immigrants gave the United States the longest name for any of its cities. In Spanish,	
is *El Pueblo de Nuestra Señora la Reina de los Angeles de Porciúncula*—Los Angeles.	30b
American cuisine now includes foods from many other traditions, from Chinese	
sweet-and-sour pork to Greek baklava. American children who enjoy to eat pizza or	28f
spaghetti or tacos think they are eating American food. Since the Germans brought	
the Christmas tree to America, every immigrant group that celebrates Christmas	
it has added something to American Christmas customs. Fiestas and serenades are	30c
common in the United States, and even New England children often want to break	
open a piñata on their birthday parties. Every summer in Washington, DC, Americans	31a
celebrate the diversity of their culture with an excited folk festival. Groups from	30g
many different cultures in America bring an equipment to produce their own foods	29e
and festivities on the national Mall, where many other Americans can enjoy them. A	29a
alien visitor would not be able to tell which songs and stories are "American," for the	
food, festivals, dances, music, and folktales of immigrant groups have became part of	28a
America's own culture.	

Van Goor and Hacker, *Developmental Exercises for The Bedford Handbook*, 9th ed. (Boston: Bedford, 2014)

28–31 | Review: Multilingual writers and ESL challenges   **117**

EXERCISE 32/33-1 ◆ The comma and unnecessary commas: Guided practice

Edit the following essay by adding commas where they are needed and removing unnecessary commas. The numbers in the margin refer to relevant rules in sections 32 and 33 of *The Bedford Handbook*, Ninth Edition. The first revision has been done for you; answers to this exercise appear in the back of this book.

Young adult dystopian literature is a popular genre with a growing fan base
worldwide; its books are characterized by degradation, totalitarian states, and   32c
dehumanization. With the release of the film version of Suzanne Collins's *The Hunger*
Games the genre has amassed a following similar to that of wizards and vampires   32b
in fiction and pop culture. Writers such as Lois Lowry and M. T. Anderson have been
producing award-winning dystopian work for years. But the wild popularity of such
writers reveals that young readers welcome the serious dark work being marketed to   32d
them. The dystopian novel takes risks and teenagers like risks. In sophisticated ways   32a
that are satisfying to young readers, these books depict pain, loss, and the anxieties of
growing up.

Dystopia is the opposite of utopia which is any system of political or social   32e
perfection an ideal place or state. Dystopia signifies regression. It is a fictional   32e
society characterized by, poverty, oppression, disease, or overcrowding. The world in   33c
a dystopian novel is recognizable as a warped version of our own; people may survive
an epic tragedy, often environmental or political, and survivors form a society, that   33e
curtails freedoms to protect citizens. A hero or heroine must triumph over terrible
odds to better the society, and restore harmony. The novels are often violent. While   33a
the violence may disturb parents teenagers want stories with weight and intensity.   32a
They want to immerse themselves in a world where there is no happy ending, a world
that challenges and shocks them and where they can see the best and the worst of
humanity.

Van Goor and Hacker, *Developmental Exercises for*
The Bedford Handbook, 9th ed. (Boston: Bedford, 2014)

EXERCISE 32/33-2 ◆ The comma

To read about this topic, see sections 32 and 33 in *The Bedford Handbook*, Ninth Edition.

A Insert commas where they are needed with coordinating conjunctions in the following sentences. If a sentence is correct, mark it "OK." Example:

Four major elements appear consistently in young adult dystopian literature, and these elements provide the framework for the novel and make the story powerful.

1. A story doesn't need to have all four elements, but the best do.

2. First, a vivid setting is essential and usually it's so clearly described that it becomes a character itself.

3. Second, the individuals or forces in control must be well developed if their motives are to be understood.

4. Third, the protagonists should be shaped by their environment but they should still possess the ability to change and adapt to new surroundings.

5. Finally, the conclusion of the book must reflect the dire circumstances that created the problems in the first place and it should feel inevitable.

B Insert commas where they are needed after an introductory element, in a series, and with coordinate adjectives. If a sentence is correct, mark it "OK." Example:

Philip Reeve's futuristic Fever Crumb trilogy consists of the books *Fever Crumb, A Web of Air,* and *Scrivener's Moon.*

6. In *Fever Crumb*, the first book, Reeve uses descriptive and sophisticated language to introduce the reader to Fever, his icy intelligent heroine.

7. The book's portrait of a dark crumbling London takes shape quickly. When Fever starts to question herself and her history, she begins to understand what's really been going on around her.

8. The author's sharp, understated humor is a welcome contrast to Fever's rational approach to life.

9. Through his skill as a wordsmith, his impeccable timing and his attention to detail, Reeve conveys the intricacies of a degenerate society.

10. Although the reason behind the rise in popularity of dystopian literature among young adults is debatable some believe it can be attributed to twenty-first-century economic and environmental crises as well as to an overall lack of optimism about the future of humanity.

Van Goor and Hacker, *Developmental Exercises for The Bedford Handbook*, 9th ed. (Boston: Bedford, 2014)

EXERCISE 32/33-3 ◆ The comma

To read about this topic, see sections 32 and 33 in *The Bedford Handbook*, Ninth Edition.

A Insert commas where they are needed and delete commas where they are not needed. If a sentence is correct, mark it "OK." Example:

The lack of complacency in the dystopian novel can be seen on the first page, often in the

first paragraph.

1. One of the earliest contributors to the young adult dystopian genre is Lois Lowry whose novel *The Giver* won the Newbery Medal in 1994. [Lowry wrote more than one novel.]

2. *The Giver* is still taught in schools alongside the older dystopian novels, *Brave New World* and *Animal Farm*.

3. *The Giver*, which has continued to appeal to young readers, caused quite a stir when it was published because of its troublesome subject matter.

4. Parents of adolescents at the time thumbed through *The Giver* with trepidation a feeling with which many readers approached the book.

5. *The Giver*'s story and its immense popularity still resonate today; in April 2012, the Minnesota Opera, based in Minneapolis, presented Susan Kander's operatic vision of *The Giver* to sold-out shows.

B Insert commas where they are needed and delete commas where they are not needed. If a sentence is correct, mark it "OK." Example:

***The Giver* features a suppressed society in which children are assigned jobs for life at the**

age of twelve, a society where people no longer know how to suffer because they cannot

feel pain or emotion.

6. Jonas the protagonist is given the role of receiver of memories.

7. As Jonas accepts memories from the current receiver, a wise old man known as the Giver he experiences love, loss, color, the sun, snow, terror, and excitement for the first time.

8. When the Giver tells Jonas the true meaning of the ceremony known as "release" the two decide to join forces to save their community.

Van Goor and Hacker, *Developmental Exercises for*
The Bedford Handbook, 9th ed. (Boston: Bedford, 2014)

32/33-3 | The comma   **121**

9. To give the memories of the past back to the community Jonas must escape to Elsewhere and leave the Giver behind to help people cope with the flood of emotion and changes to come.

10. Although subject matter such as this can be challenging for young readers, Lowry has said "Pretending that there are no choices to be made—reading only books, for example, which are cheery and safe and nice—is a prescription for disaster for the young."

Van Goor and Hacker, *Developmental Exercises for*
The Bedford Handbook, 9th ed. (Boston: Bedford, 2014)

EXERCISE 32/33-4 ◆ The comma

To read about this topic, see sections 32 and 33 in *The Bedford Handbook*, Ninth Edition.

Edit the following paragraphs to correct the use of commas. The first revision has been done for you. You should add ten more commas.

Feed, M. T. Anderson's award-winning dystopian novel for young adults, focuses on modern anxieties about the changing world. Specifically the role of technology acts as the text's central theme. The book depicts a world in which most of its inhabitants live with a "feed" a microchip implanted in their brains. The chip connects owners to the "feednet" which allows instant advertising and manipulation of the owner's mind by corporations. The "feednet" evidently a futuristic version of the Internet, acts as a constant force and distraction. This scenario is not unlike that facing the modern teen who must now navigate a world of information through computers, smartphones, iPods and other portable devices. Anderson recognizes that teenagers are the age group most likely to ask "What does this all mean?" He thinks teens are well equipped to think about the effects that advances in technology might have on society and to ask and contemplate serious questions. Anderson believes that to engage today's young people a writer must connect with what's on their minds. Teens, like adults should be viewed as a smart curious audience for good literature.

Van Goor and Hacker, *Developmental Exercises for*
The Bedford Handbook, 9th ed. (Boston: Bedford, 2014)

32/33-4 | The comma   **123**

EXERCISE 32/33-5 ◆ Unnecessary commas

To read about this topic, see sections 32 and 33 in *The Bedford Handbook*, Ninth Edition.

Each of the following sentences contains one unnecessary comma. Delete the comma that is not needed. Example:

Another characteristic of the current dystopian trend/is the rise of the heroine.

1. The popularity of Suzanne Collins's *The Hunger Games*, can be seen as a counterpoint to the popularity of Stephenie Meyer's Twilight series.

2. While the Twilight books feature a melodramatic Bella Swan, as their heroine, Collins's female protagonist, Katniss, is too busy surviving to cry for help.

3. Many readers, young and old, criticized Bella's passivity, and her need to be saved.

4. Meeting Katniss, readers see a resemblance to the strong female protagonists of the fantasy genre, such as Hermione in the Harry Potter books and Lyra, in Philip Pullman's His Dark Materials trilogy.

5. Katniss refuses to adhere to the rules enforced by the Capitol, and is determined to prove that, in the end, the authorities cannot control her.

6. She is a heroine that young adult readers of both sexes can admire, for, she is strong-willed, passionate, intelligent, and tough.

7. When tributes are chosen for the Capitol's annual Hunger Games, a horrific event held to remind the Districts of their powerlessness, Katniss puts her life at risk, and volunteers to be a tribute in place of her younger sister.

8. Though Katniss doesn't have the extensive training that many of the other tributes have, her conviction and compassion, ultimately set her apart.

9. She remains, one of the few participants who does not have to resort to brutality to prove that she is just as strong as, if not stronger than, her savage contenders.

10. Katniss proves to be the type of protagonist, who, like Bella, will continue to win fans and whom we will continue to see in young adult literature.

Van Goor and Hacker, *Developmental Exercises for The Bedford Handbook*, 9th ed. (Boston: Bedford, 2014)

EXERCISE 32/33-6 ◆ Unnecessary commas

To read about this topic, see sections 32 and 33 in *The Bedford Handbook*, Ninth Edition.

One sentence in each of the following pairs is correctly punctuated. Circle the letter of the correct sentence and edit the incorrect sentence. Example:

(a.) **Writers of young adult dystopian literature depict heroes and heroines who, while flawed and imperfect, possess the morals and the tenacity of the best role models.**

b. **Though these characters make mistakes and break rules/their motives and their determination are a reflection of their desire to do good.**

1. a. Their audacity, which we see in Katniss in *The Hunger Games*, reflects the individuality, and self-assertion portrayed in more and more young female protagonists.

   b. Increasingly in young adult fiction, the love interest story line is subordinate to the heroine's moral dilemma.

2. a. Dystopian works tend to be less angst-filled and romanticized than other young adult works like, the Twilight series.

   b. Despite being desperately in love, most protagonists don't dwell on appearances or emotions because they're too busy trying to save the world.

3. a. Scott Westerfeld's Uglies series imagines a postapocalyptic world in which all teenagers are ugly, until radical surgery at age sixteen makes them into supermodel "pretties."

   b. Published in 2005, the first novel, *Uglies*, was admired by girls and young women because it allowed them to talk about the pressure they felt about their looks, an age-old anxiety.

4. a. The author's depiction of the consequences that can arise from body alteration for the sake of beauty gives the book plenty of complex topics for readers to consider.

   b. The fact that *Uglies* and the books that followed it were wildly popular, proves that girls and young women want to read about challenging topics that they can relate to.

5. a. When teenagers can talk about the pressure to conform to a standard of beauty, they have a better chance of accepting themselves as they are.

   b. The dystopian novel, like its science fiction counterpart, has the power to examine, and change the way our society functions.

EXERCISE 32/33-7 ◆ The comma and unnecessary commas: Guided review

Edit the following paragraphs by adding commas where they are needed and removing commas where they are not needed. The numbers in the margin refer to relevant rules in sections 32 and 33 of *The Bedford Handbook*, Ninth Edition. The first revision has been done for you.

A good dystopian novel is driven by a resistance to conformity, a classic theme   32e

of young adult life that continues into later life. Dystopian literature magnifies

teen issues such as bullying, and the struggle to make independent decisions. Some   33a

critics think the popularity of this genre is a reflection of the pressures of a changing

economy, growing concerns about the environment and the bleak picture for the   32c

future. While these topics are a likely source of some of the genre's inspiration the core   32b

themes of dystopian literature embody the struggles of human existence, concepts and

concerns that do not go away over time.

The degenerate societies depicted in young adult dystopian literature, full of

chaos and corruption make readers consider and question the state of their world, and   32e, 33a

their role in it. Teenagers are a group experiencing change and developmental growth,   33e

that comes about by being exposed to new and challenging situations. They must learn

to face the challenges of becoming adults, just as their protagonists must.

From Lowry's Jonas to Collins's Katniss readers see an evolution of strong   32b

writing by authors unafraid to take risks. These authors want to give today's young

people a voice and, the means to understand the world around them.   33h

Dystopian novels clearly have something to tell us about what occupies and

excites the minds of today's teenagers. Considering that adults are also reading them   32b

these works are likely to teach everyone something meaningful about the world.

Young readers can rejoice that they're getting books they deserve, with protagonists of

integrity, and ideas of real consequence.   33a

Van Goor and Hacker, *Developmental Exercises for The Bedford Handbook,* 9th ed. (Boston: Bedford, 2014)

EXERCISE 34-1 ◆ The semicolon: Guided practice

Edit the following paragraphs to correct problems with the use of semicolons. The numbers in the margin refer to relevant rules in section 34 of *The Bedford Handbook*, Ninth Edition. The first revision has been done for you; answers to this exercise appear in the back of this book.

When Cheryl Toussaint came in second in a race she had never planned to run**/,** she started on a road that led to the Olympics and a world record.   34d

Cheryl began running almost by accident one day when she went to watch a city-sponsored track meet in Brooklyn, New York. During the preliminaries, the officials announced an "open" race, it was one that anyone could enter. Cheryl wanted   34a
to enter; but she was dressed in a skirt and sandals. Four things made her run; one   34d, 34d
friend traded shoes with her, another let her borrow jeans, several called her "chicken" if she didn't run, and one girl dared her to run. Coming in second in that race led this teenager to many places, including Munich, Germany, Toronto, Canada, and Montreal,   34c
Canada.

There were, however, many races to run and lessons to learn. Cheryl joined the all-female Atoms Track Club, and she began training under Coach Fred Thompson. Like most coaches, Fred had his own way of testing newcomers. He watched new runners carefully, however, he gave them no special attention. Instead, he just gave   34b
them orders one after another. He would tell Cheryl to run laps, perform exercises, and repeat practice starts, at the same time, he would never comment on how she   34a
performed. If the newcomers endured the hard, time-consuming workouts without encouragement or praise; Thompson was sure that they were ready for real coaching.   34d

Cheryl quit after two months, for six more months, she stayed away from the   34a
club. During that time, she thought about her attitude toward work, her poor record at school, her pleasure in running, and her lack of goals. When she returned to the club;   34d
Thompson welcomed her back. Coach Thompson knew how special Cheryl was, he not   34a
only convinced her she was college material but also pushed her to achieve the highest goal of the amateur athlete—competing in the Olympics.

Van Goor and Hacker, *Developmental Exercises for*
The Bedford Handbook, 9th ed. (Boston: Bedford, 2014)

34-1 | The semicolon: Guided practice   **127**

EXERCISE 34-2 ◆ The semicolon

To read about this topic, see section 34 in *The Bedford Handbook*, Ninth Edition.

Add semicolons in the five word groups that need them; mark the other word groups "OK." Example:

> **Cheryl Toussaint's first official run was an indication of her character and determination;**
>
> **no one could find fault with her effort.**

1. Cheryl's first official run—at a cross-country meet on Long Island—would certainly have impressed any coach every person watching was astounded by her perseverance.

2. Coach Thompson had warned her not to start too fast but to stay with the pack. "Just try to finish," he said.

3. Too excited to follow his directions, Cheryl took off at top speed at the starting gun, moreover, she did not slow down even after she was a hundred yards in front of everyone else.

4. Cheryl kept that distance for most of the run, she did not allow herself any slack.

5. Then, with only a hundred yards to go, Cheryl gave out, she collapsed and fell down.

6. Immediately, she got to her knees and started crawling. She crawled toward the finish line, not toward the grassy area where runners who left the race were supposed to go.

7. She stood up, staggered a little farther, and fell again. Once more she started crawling.

8. Not able to get to her feet again, Cheryl continued to crawl, after all, she was nearly at the finish line.

9. She had almost reached the finish line when another runner passed her and won the race.

10. "I knew at that moment," said her coach, "that this girl was going to be something special." Her coach was right.

Van Goor and Hacker, *Developmental Exercises for The Bedford Handbook*, 9th ed. (Boston: Bedford, 2014)

EXERCISE 34-3 ◆ The semicolon

To read about this topic, see section 34 in *The Bedford Handbook*, Ninth Edition.

Each of the following sentences contains two semicolons but should have only one. Delete the incorrect one and replace it with other punctuation if necessary. Example:

> No one else had ever seen anything special in Cheryl, who had never shown any ambition; her teachers had labeled her a "slow learner" long before she got to high school.

1. Cheryl had to beg her teachers to allow her to take college preparatory courses; they were sure she would fail; no matter how hard she tried.

2. Coach Thompson did many things for Cheryl; including coaching track, prodding her about schoolwork, encouraging good eating habits, and insisting that she think about college; most important of all, he gave her faith in herself.

3. All of the runners knew that if they made qualifying times; Coach Thompson would see to it that they were entered in the national meets; however, they also knew that if they did not qualify, they were off the team.

4. Cheryl soon discovered that she had to schedule her time; or she would fail at school or at track or at both; thinking about Coach Thompson, she began to care.

5. By the time Cheryl graduated from high school, she was an A student; this "slow learner" received an academic scholarship to New York University; although she had once thought only an athletic scholarship was possible.

Van Goor and Hacker, *Developmental Exercises for The Bedford Handbook,* 9th ed. (Boston: Bedford, 2014)

34-3 | The semicolon   **129**

EXERCISE 34-4 ◆ The semicolon: Guided review

Edit the following paragraphs to correct problems with the use of semicolons. The numbers in the margin refer to relevant rules in section 34 of *The Bedford Handbook*, Ninth Edition. The first revision has been done for you.

Every runner dreams of winning both individual and relay medals at the Olympics̷; in 1972, Cheryl Toussaint was no exception. When she did not qualify   34a

for the individual 800-meter finals; she pinned her hopes on the relay race. Her   34d

teammates on the American team were ready: Mabel Ferguson, Madeline Jackson, and Kathy Hammond. The relay was Cheryl's last chance to win a medal, unfortunately, it   34b

seemed that everything was against her.

Cheryl began the third leg of the qualifying heat with runners ahead of her. Then a runner in front of her fell. As Cheryl dashed around her, another runner stepped on the heel of Cheryl's left shoe, so Cheryl was running with her shoe half on and half off. She needed to stop and pull the shoe on, but she knew two things: She would lose valuable time, and this was her team's last chance to qualify for the finals. She kept running, very soon the shoe flew up in the air. Cheryl wondered whether   34a

the shoe would hit anyone, whether TV viewers could see her bare foot, and whether people in the stands had noticed. But she ran on, passing the other runners. Her team qualified for the finals that day, and in the finals Cheryl and her teammates won silver medals.

Cheryl remembered her very first run in Brooklyn, in which she hadn't even known how to start, her first "real" race, in which she'd crawled to the finish line, and   34c

the Olympic 800-meter individual run in which she'd failed to qualify. She could laugh about all those memories now, for she and her teammates were Olympic medalists.

Back home, Cheryl kept to her plans: graduating from college (with a B+ average), getting a job in the Federal Reserve Bank's management training program, and training for the next Olympics. She knew that nothing would ever mean as much to her again as track, the Atoms, and Coach Thompson had meant her success was   34a

also theirs.

Van Goor and Hacker, *Developmental Exercises for The Bedford Handbook*, 9th ed. (Boston: Bedford, 2014)

EXERCISE 35-1 ◆ The colon: Guided practice

In the following paragraph, insert colons where they are needed and delete any improperly used colons. The numbers in the margin refer to relevant rules in section 35 of *The Bedford Handbook*, Ninth Edition. The first revision has been done for you; answers to this exercise appear in the back of this book.

In 1951, Althea Gibson broke the color barrier in women's tennis and became admired all over the world. No one who knew her as a teenager would have predicted her success. By the time Althea Gibson reached her teens, her record showed three indications of trouble/: running away from home, dropping out of school, and losing   35a

the one job she had been able to find. To survive in her neighborhood, Althea depended on: a small welfare allowance, occasional handouts, and plain old luck. She listed   35c

her skills as the following, good bowler, great two-on-two basketball player, and fast   35a

paddleball player. Even after she began playing tennis and moving in upper-class Harlem society, she resented the efforts of the society ladies to improve her. They busied themselves with tasks such as: correcting her manners and restricting her   35c

behavior. Looking back, she summed up her earlier attitude she said she hadn't been   35a

ready to study about "how to be a fine lady." At eighteen, she finally got: a waitressing   35c

job, a congenial roommate, and a good friend.

Van Goor and Hacker, *Developmental Exercises for*
The Bedford Handbook, 9th ed. (Boston: Bedford, 2014)

35-1 | The colon: Guided practice   **131**

EXERCISE 35-2 ◆ The colon

To read about this topic, see section 35 in *The Bedford Handbook*, Ninth Edition.

In the following sentences, insert colons where they can be effectively used. Example:

> In 1957, Althea Gibson won the women's title at the most prestigious tennis tournament in
>
> the world: Wimbledon.

1. Althea Gibson broke the color barrier in women's tennis she was the first black female player to compete in national championships.

2. Two tennis-playing doctors opened their homes to her so she could finish high school and go to college Dr. Hubert A. Eaton of Wilmington, North Carolina, and Dr. Robert W. Johnson of Lynchburg, Virginia.

3. Her life in a southern high school was not pleasant; if she had written a book about it, she could have titled it *Misfit, A Yankee Woman in a Southern School*.

4. Besides tennis, Althea's other love was music the drums, the chorus, and especially the saxophone.

5. Her friend Sugar Ray Robinson firmly advised her to go to college "No matter what you want to do, tennis or music or what, you'll be better at it if you get some education."

Van Goor and Hacker, *Developmental Exercises for The Bedford Handbook*, 9th ed. (Boston: Bedford, 2014)

EXERCISE 35-3 ◆ The colon

To read about this topic, see section 35 in *The Bedford Handbook*, Ninth Edition.

In the following paragraphs, the italicized words indicate where two parts of a sentence come together. Decide whether the sentence needs a colon to join these parts. If it does, insert one. If it does not, mark the spot "OK." The first sentence has been marked for you. Hint: You will need very few colons.

OK

Althea Gibson began playing *tennis when* she was a young teenager in the 1940s. In just over a decade, she *became one* of the world's greatest women tennis players.

The tennis world began to notice her after only a few years of amateur *play she* was winning women's singles meets one after the other. In 1950 and the years immediately *following, she* became more and more famous. By 1957, Althea Gibson, the rising young tennis star, was well known on both sides of the *Atlantic she* was the most respected woman player in Britain and America. In both countries, she won the national women's singles title two years in a row: 1957 and 1958. The British meet, which is *called Wimbledon,* is generally regarded *as the* unofficial world championship meet. Gibson also played on the US team at other major meets, *including the* Wightman Cup meet. That meet is a special British-American *meet that* pits US women against British women. When Althea Gibson was on the US team, the United States won.

Gibson's retirement from tennis in 1958 *was a* complete surprise to her fans. What reason did she give for her retirement? She had *decided to* become a professional golfer!

Van Goor and Hacker, *Developmental Exercises for The Bedford Handbook,* 9th ed. (Boston: Bedford, 2014)

35-3 | The colon **133**

EXERCISE 35-4 ◆ The colon: Guided review

In the following paragraph, insert colons where they are needed and delete any improperly used colons. The numbers in the margin refer to relevant rules in section 35 of *The Bedford Handbook*, Ninth Edition. The first revision has been done for you.

When the Eatons of North Carolina invited Althea Gibson to move into their home for the school year, she hesitated. Northerner Althea had one major fear/: white southerners. She decided to go in spite of her fears. At the Eatons' house, Althea had to get used to: wearing skirts, obeying rules, and getting along with people. She was expected to listen to adult conversations and join in with well-chosen comments. At the time, Althea considered these requirements to be serious disadvantages. However, there were also advantages to life with the Eatons, such as: regular meals, a room of her own, an allowance, and unlimited use of the doctor's private tennis court. School presented one overwhelming social problem Althea could not make friends with either boys or girls. The boys may have resented her athletic prowess and her self-confidence. The girls considered her a tomboy. Years later Althea still recalled their taunts "She's no lady" and "Look at her throwing that ball just like a man." Even the singing instructor added to her woes. When he placed her in the tenor section to make the chorus sound better, the other girls in the chorus could not control their giggles. Some people even made fun of her tennis, but her tenacity paid off. Before she had finished high school, Florida A&M University had offered her a scholarship. Althea had been right to expect problems if she lived in the South, but she had not anticipated what the problems would be. If she had put the story of those high school years into a book, she could have titled it *The Unexpected, Problems Are Not Always What They Seem.*

35a
35c
35c
35a
35a
35b

Van Goor and Hacker, *Developmental Exercises for The Bedford Handbook*, 9th ed. (Boston: Bedford, 2014)

EXERCISE 36-1 ◆ The apostrophe: Guided practice

In the following paragraphs, add apostrophes where they are missing and delete or correct them where they are misused. The numbers in the margin refer to relevant rules in section 36 of *The Bedford Handbook*, Ninth Edition. The first revision has been done for you; answers to this exercise appear in the back of this book.

During the 1990 troubles in Panama, American television and newspaper reporters had an exciting piece of news. They reported that for the first time American female soldiers had been engaged in actual combat. Acting as her ~~soldiers~~ soldiers' leader, Captain Linda Bray led her troops into combat. Names of two additional women who were involved in combat, Staff Sergeant April Hanley and Private First Class Christina Proctor, were reported in the newspapers. Their's were the only names reported, although other women also took part in the fighting.

36a

36e

It wasn't the first time an American woman had fought in an American battle, but its not likely that many people are aware of that fact. The Civil War had its female fighters too. Loreta Janeta Velazquez fought for the Confederates' in the Civil War after her husbands death. Like many other women whose husbands were killed in that war, she must have asked herself, "Whose going to take his place in battle?" The decision to fight was her's alone. Someone is sure to ask how that was possible, especially in those days. Military identification was not very sophisticated in the 1860s. Someones willingness to fight was that person's major qualification, and each fighting unit needed to replace it's losses as fast as possible. Velazquez simply disguised herself in mens clothing, found a troop needing replacements, and joined the fight. Loreta Janeta Velazquez was Linda Brays Civil War predecessor.

36c

36e

36a

36c

36e

36b

36e

36a

36a

Van Goor and Hacker, *Developmental Exercises for*
The Bedford Handbook, 9th ed. (Boston: Bedford, 2014)

36-1 | The apostrophe: Guided practice   **135**

EXERCISE 36-2 ◆ The apostrophe

To read about this topic, see section 36 in *The Bedford Handbook*, Ninth Edition.

A Each of the following sentences has two words containing apostrophes. Only one of the apostrophes is used correctly in each sentence. Delete or move the other apostrophe. Example:

Further back in American history, one woman's soldiering had made her famous; no one

hers.

has yet had a story to match ~~her's.~~
⌃

1. Deborah Sampson never dreamed that she would someday fight in battles' for American independence, much less that the battles' outcomes might depend on her.

2. Because her parents' income was not enough to support their children, her parents' sent Deborah to live with relatives in another town.

3. Later she was sent to live in a foster family with ten sons'; the sons' acceptance of her was wholehearted, and one son became her fiancé when she grew up.

4. The Revolutionary War was'nt over when news of his death reached Deborah; she wasn't long in making a major decision.

5. Determined that his place should become her's, she enlisted under a man's name.

B The following sentences contain no apostrophes. Add any that are needed and make any necessary corrections in spelling. If a sentence is correct, mark it "OK." Example:

Who's   who's
~~Whose~~ to say ~~whos~~ right about Deborah Sampson's decision?
⌃   ⌃

6. If men have the right to fight for their beliefs, should women have the right to fight for theirs?

7. Its clear that Deborah Sampson thought so; she enlisted twice to fight for hers.

8. On her first attempt, Sampson enlisted almost at the end of the day—and was discovered before its end arrived.

9. Though drinking was not a habit of hers, she spent her first evening as a soldier copying other new soldiers behavior.

10. Coming to the aid of this very noisy, very drunk, and very sick "buddy" of theirs, they soon were asking, "Whose this?"

Van Goor and Hacker, *Developmental Exercises for The Bedford Handbook*, 9th ed. (Boston: Bedford, 2014)

EXERCISE 36-3 ◆ The apostrophe

To read about this topic, see section 36 in *The Bedford Handbook*, Ninth Edition.

Circle the correct form of the words in parentheses. The first sentence has been done for you.

Loreta Velazquez was not the only woman (who's /(whose)) help was used during the Civil War, nor was being a foot soldier the only way women served in that war.

She was not in combat, but Mary Walker, then in her (thirties / thirty's), served in the Union army. She served with such distinction that she became the first woman to receive the Medal of Honor, the (military's / militarys') highest-ranking medal. It is awarded only to members of the armed (forces / force's) and only for gallantry in action.

Mary (Walker's / Walkers) specialty was surgery. Just as shocking as her profession—the role of military surgeon was not (everyone's / everyones') idea of the proper role for a woman in the 1860s—were Dr. Walker's opinions on how women should dress. She said that women (shouldn't / should'nt) wear tight corsets because such corsets were injurious to (women's / womens') health. She even considered long skirts unhealthy. She felt so strongly on the subject of women's attire that she was determined to wear long pants. Army (regulations / regulations') did not permit such attire for a woman. (Who's / Whose) permission was required for her to do so? Special permission from the US Congress was required, but Dr. Mary Walker finally won that battle of the Civil War.

She did not live to see the end of her final battle, however. After the war, she went back to her private practice of medicine and began fighting for a constitutional amendment to allow women to vote. Congress passed the Nineteenth Amendment in 1920. Unfortunately, Mary Walker died before (its / it's) adoption.

Van Goor and Hacker, *Developmental Exercises for The Bedford Handbook*, 9th ed. (Boston: Bedford, 2014)

36-3 | The apostrophe **137**

EXERCISE 36-4 ◆ The apostrophe: Guided review

In the following paragraph, add apostrophes where they are missing and delete or correct them where they are misused. The numbers in the margin refer to relevant rules in section 36 of *The Bedford Handbook*, Ninth Edition. The first revision has been done for you.

Deborah Sampson, who fought in the American Revolution, fulfilled her light

infantryman duties pretending to be a private named Robert Shurtlieff. To ~~anyones~~ *anyone's*   36b

questions about where he was based, this private said, "West Point." Sampson's first

enlistment lasted less than a day, but her second enlistment was different. It lasted

until the wars end, when along with many others she was honorably discharged from   36a

the Continental army on October 23, 1783. Throughout her service, it was everyones   36b

opinion that she was an excellent soldier. Her officers reports on her were always good.   36a

Wounded twice, she outwitted the doctors' and returned to her unit undetected; but   36e

when she came down with "the fevers," a doctor discovered the secret that until then

had been her's alone. (Many of the distinctions among different illnesses that produce   36e

fevers—from typhoid to influenza—were not yet known; if patients had a high fever

and it's accompanying discomforts for very long, they were diagnosed as having   36e

"the fevers.") Its no surprise that when her secret was finally revealed, her superior   36c

officers couldnt believe it. Dressed in women's clothes, she was escorted to separate   36c

quarters not by the military police but by her superior officers. Many years later, at

Paul Reveres' suggestion, she donned the uniform again and went on speaking tours'   36a, 36e

to raise much-needed money for her family and to secure a monthly pension from the

army she had once served.

Van Goor and Hacker, *Developmental Exercises for*
The Bedford Handbook, 9th ed. (Boston: Bedford, 2014)

EXERCISE 37-1 ◆ Quotation marks: Guided practice

Edit the following sentences to correct the use of quotation marks and of punctuation with quotation marks. The numbers in the margin refer to relevant rules in section 37 of *The Bedford Handbook*, Ninth Edition. Answers to this exercise appear in the back of this book. Example:

The parents watched as the doctor bandaged the boy's eyes. "For the love of

God, what can we do ?" asked the father.   37e

1. The doctor answered "You can do nothing but pray."   37e

2. When the bandages were removed and the shades were opened to let in the   37e

   bright sunlight, the doctor asked, "What do you see"?

3. "Nothing," said the boy. I see nothing.   37a

4. The village priest said "I have recently seen a remarkable school." He had just   37e

   returned from a trip to Paris.

5. "In this school, he added blind students are taught to read."   37a

6. "You didn't say "read," did you?" asked the boy's father.   37b

7. The boy responded to the priest's words as if they were a trick of some kind   37e

   "Now you are joking with me. How can such a thing be possible?"

8. The boy, Louis, thought it would be "great fun" to visit that school someday.   37f

9. His father promised "We will go soon, Louis."   37e

10. And so it happened that ten-year-old Louis Braille entered the National   37d

    Institute for Blind Youth and began the long effort to erase the fear people had

    of even the word blind.

Van Goor and Hacker, *Developmental Exercises for*
The Bedford Handbook, 9th ed. (Boston: Bedford, 2014)

37-1 | Quotation marks: Guided practice **139**

EXERCISE 37-2 ◆ Quotation marks

To read about this topic, see section 37 in *The Bedford Handbook*, Ninth Edition.

Change each indirect quotation into a direct quotation, using correct punctuation and deleting or changing words as necessary. Example:

The doctor told them not to look for miracles.

The doctor said, "Do not look for miracles."

_____

1. The doctor added that in all probability their son would never see again.

_____

_____

2. Mr. Braille exclaimed that he had seen blind students at the institute making their own clothes and shoes.

_____

_____

3. The inventor of the raised-dot system of writing used in the military told Louis to experiment all he wished but not to set his hopes too high.

_____

_____

4. When his old friends in the village saw him with his stylus and paper, they asked him if he was still punching away at it.

_____

_____

5. Louis asked the government official if he was blind and if he understood what it was like not to see.

_____

_____

Van Goor and Hacker, *Developmental Exercises for The Bedford Handbook*, 9th ed. (Boston: Bedford, 2014)

EXERCISE 37-3 ◆ Quotation marks

To read about this topic, see section 37 in *The Bedford Handbook*, Ninth Edition.

In the following sentences, insert needed quotation marks and punctuation used with quotation marks. If a sentence is correct, mark it "OK." Example:

> **One of Braille's students wrote, "Attending his classes was a pleasure to enjoy rather than a duty to fulfill."**

1. Louis Braille asked the inventor of the raised-dot system of writing a serious question "Do you think it would be possible to change the symbols in some way, to reduce them in size?"

2. Barbier, the inventor of the system, replied "Of course. Anything is possible."

3. "I have hoped" said the founder of the institute "that this school would be a bright torch held aloft to bring light to the blind."

4. "I am going to instruct the teachers to begin using your system in the classroom," said the institute director. "You must understand, though, that your method has not yet been proved."

5. Louis Braille wanted a system so complete that blind people could read and write the words and music to a song like the Marseillaise, the French national anthem.

Van Goor and Hacker, *Developmental Exercises for*
The Bedford Handbook, 9th ed. (Boston: Bedford, 2014)

EXERCISE 37-4 ◆ Quotation marks: Guided review

Edit the following paragraphs to correct the use of quotation marks and of punctuation used with quotation marks. The numbers in the margin refer to relevant rules in section 37 of *The Bedford Handbook*, Ninth Edition. The first correction has been made for you.

Louis Braille entered the National Institute for Blind Youth in Paris when he

was ten. At twelve, he was already experimenting with a system of raised dots on

paper known as "night-~~writing~~," *writing,"* which was used by the military. Institute teachers   37e

decided that night-writing was impractical, but Louis became proficient at it. When   37e

Charles Barbier, inventor of the system, visited the institute, Louis told him "Your   37a

symbols are too large and too complicated. Impressed, Barbier encouraged him and   37f

said that "since Louis was blind himself, he might discover the magic key that had

eluded his teachers."

    Louis Braille wanted a system that could transcribe everything from a textbook   37c

on science to a poem like Heinrich Heine's Loreley. At fifteen, he had worked out his

own system of six dots arranged in various patterns. "Read to me," he said to one of his   37e

teachers, and I will take down your words." As the teacher read, Louis punched dots

onto his paper and then read the passage back without error. The teacher exclaimed,   37e

"Remarkable"! Government officials, not impressed enough to take any action, said   37e

simply that Braille should be encouraged. "You didn't say "encouraged," did you?"   37b

asked Braille. He wanted official acceptance, not simply encouragement. "The system

has proved itself," said Louis. We have been using it for five years now."   37e

    For most people, the word Braille itself now means simply a system of   37d

reading and writing used by blind people; for blind people, it means freedom and

independence. Braille himself died before his system was recognized beyond the

institute. The plaque on the house of his birth, however, records the world's recognition

of his work with these words: He opened the doors of knowledge to all those who   37a

cannot see.

Van Goor and Hacker, *Developmental Exercises for The Bedford Handbook*, 9th ed. (Boston: Bedford, 2014)

EXERCISE 38-1 ◆ End punctuation: Guided practice

Supply end punctuation—period, question mark, or exclamation point—as needed in the following paragraphs. The numbers in the margin refer to relevant rules in section 38 of *The Bedford Handbook*, Ninth Edition. The first and last revisions have been done for you; answers to this exercise appear in the back of this book.

After Louis Braille invented his new system that would allow blind people to

read and write, he tested it thoroughly. Students and faculty of the National Institute   38a
                              ^
for Blind Youth were excited at how easily they could master it. They encouraged

Louis to demonstrate the system to the French educational authorities, who made the

rules for the institute Louis agreed to do so   38a, 38a

When Louis held the demonstration, all went well What excitement he and his   38a

friends felt But the authorities would not recommend that the institute adopt Louis's   38c

new system Why didn't the French authorities recognize the advantages of Braille's   38a

system Did they have a vested interest in the old system of teaching the blind Or a   38b, 38b

real doubt about the new system Whatever their reasons, they delayed the pleasures   38b

of reading for thousands of people In addition, a new director, Dr. Pignier, even   38a

outlawed the use of the system at the institute for four years   38a

Although unhappy and disheartened, Braille never gave up; he knew his system

would enable the blind to read.   38a
                        ^

EXERCISE 38-2 ◆ End punctuation

To read about this topic, see section 38 in *The Bedford Handbook*, Ninth Edition.

Supply end punctuation—period, question mark, or exclamation point—for each of the following sentences. At least one sentence of each pair is a question. Example:

> a. **Louis asked if he could demonstrate his technique at the institute.**
>
> b. **Louis asked, "May I demonstrate my technique at the ~~institute"~~** institute?"

1. a. What Louis had figured out was a new code

   b. What had Louis figured out

2. a. What should he do about teaching it

   b. What to do about teaching it was the next decision to make

3. a. Who could help him test the system was another question

   b. Who could help him test the system

4. a. How extraordinary it was that a leatherworker's son should have such talent

   b. How was it that he had such extraordinary talent

5. a. Why did he never give up, either as a child or as an adult

   b. Why he never gave up, either as a child or as an adult, puzzled many of his friends

Van Goor and Hacker, *Developmental Exercises for The Bedford Handbook*, 9th ed. (Boston: Bedford, 2014)

EXERCISE 38-3 ◆ End punctuation: Guided review

Supply appropriate end punctuation—period, question mark, or exclamation point—in the following paragraphs. The numbers in the margin refer to relevant rules in section 38 of *The Bedford Handbook*, Ninth
Edition. The first revision has been done for you.

Braille's reading and writing system depended on a group of six dots. He called
this group a "cell." He conceived of the cell as three rows with space for two dots on
each row. But he did not have to put two dots on each row, and he did not have to use
all three rows. Figuring it this way, Braille counted sixty-three possible arrangements   38a
for the dots. Using these possibilities, Braille worked out an alphabet. Then he added
punctuation marks and numerals. But he still was not satisfied. There was something
else that he wanted to do.

Braille knew very well that blindness does not keep someone from becoming
proficient at a particular skill. Like many other blind people, Braille himself was an
accomplished musician. As a young boy at the National Institute for Blind Youth, he
had learned to play several instruments. But he could play only by ear Louis Braille   38a
wanted to be able to read music, play what he read, and then write music that other
musicians could read and play.

When Braille was only fifteen, he devised a way to write music using his six-dot
cell. As soon as he knew it was workable, he wanted a piano of his own to try it on. By
saving his small salary, he was able to buy a piano. Next he wanted lessons Paris had   38a
many good music teachers. Braille took lessons from some of the best and then began
to teach piano and violoncello at the institute. He also gave frequent piano recitals
throughout Paris.

When he knew he was good on the piano, Braille said it was time to play
something else "God's music," the church organ, was what he wanted to learn. With   38a
great effort he learned to manage the foot pedals, the double keyboard, and the rows of
stops Saint-Nicholas-des-Champs church hired him as its organist. However, Braille   38a
found himself so busy thinking about stops and pedals that he couldn't keep up with
the service at first. Did he resign Of course not Braille simply became so familiar with   38b, 38c

the music that he did not have to think about it and could follow the church service as it went along Louis Braille may have been the first blind organist in Paris, but he was not the last. In Braille's lifetime, the institute's music director placed more than fifty blind organists in the city.

38a

Many people have wondered where Braille got the idea of adapting his new system to music. Did it come from one of his teachers Or one of his friends Or from his own mind? However it happened, he adapted the Braille system for music, and again Braille opened a new world to the blind. What an extraordinary gift this was Except for sight itself, could anyone have given blind musicians a greater gift

38b, 38b

38c

38b

Van Goor and Hacker, *Developmental Exercises for The Bedford Handbook*, 9th ed. (Boston: Bedford, 2014)

Note: For exercises 39-1 to 39-4 and the review exercise on page 152, you will need to refer to the following poem.

The New Colossus
by Emma Lazarus

Not like the brazen giant of Greek fame,

With conquering limbs astride from land to land;

Here at our sea-washed, sunset gates shall stand

A mighty woman with a torch, whose flame

Is the imprisoned lightning, and her name

Mother of Exiles. From her beacon hand

Glows world-wide welcome; her mild eyes command

The air-bridged harbor that twin cities frame.

"Keep, ancient lands, your storied pomp!" cries she

With silent lips. "Give me your tired, your poor,

Your huddled masses yearning to breathe free,

The wretched refuse of your teeming shore,

Send these, the homeless, tempest-tost to me,

I lift my lamp beside the golden door."

Van Goor and Hacker, *Developmental Exercises for*
The Bedford Handbook, 9th ed. (Boston: Bedford, 2014)

39 | Other punctuation marks   **147**

EXERCISE 39-1 ◆ Other punctuation marks: Guided practice

Edit the following paragraphs for correct use of the dash, parentheses, brackets, the ellipsis mark, and the slash. Refer to the poem "The New Colossus" (p. 147) as necessary. The numbers in the margin refer to relevant rules in section 39 of *The Bedford Handbook*, Ninth Edition. The first revision has been done for you; answers to this exercise appear in the back of this book.

The most famous woman in America is Miss Liberty͵ a 450,000-pound, 154-foot   39a

resident of New York City. For people all over the world, the Statue of Liberty

symbolizes America. Yet the idea for the statue came not from America, England, or

even New York itself, but from France. Three men can claim credit for the construction   39a

of Miss Liberty: 1. Frédéric-Auguste Bartholdi, sculptor; 2. Alexandre-Gustave Eiffel,   39b

structural engineer; and 3. Richard Morris Hunt, architect. France gave the statue to

the United States, and the United States provided the pedestal—on which it stands.   39a

Two Americans contributed significantly to the statue. The first was Joseph

Pulitzer, then owner and publisher of the *New York World* (and a Russian immigrant).   39b

He led several fundraising efforts and urged every American to give what he/she could   39e

to help build the pedestal. The second American who contributed significantly was

Emma Lazarus. She wrote the famous lines on the bronze plaque inside the statue.

Her three-word title "The New Colossus" (which means "huge statue") alludes to a

statue built in the harbor of Rhodes in ancient Greece. The most quoted lines from

"The New Colossus" are probably these: "Give me your tired, your poor, / Your huddled

masses yearning to breathe free."

Van Goor and Hacker, *Developmental Exercises for
The Bedford Handbook*, 9th ed. (Boston: Bedford, 2014)

EXERCISE 39-2 ◆ Other punctuation marks

To read about this topic, see section 39 in *The Bedford Handbook*, Ninth Edition.

Edit the following sentences by using the punctuation indicated in brackets. Refer to the poem "The New Colossus" (p. 147) as necessary. Example:

Bartholdi's Statue of Liberty better known in France as Liberty Enlightening the World celebrated ideals that France and America shared. [Dashes]

1. The American Revolution celebrated liberty. The French added two more words to form the battle cry of the French Revolution, "Liberty, Equality, and Fraternity." [Dash]

2. Emma Lazarus understood Bartholdi's desire to demonstrate this shared ideal. In her opening line, "Not like the brazen giant of Greek fame" (the Colossus of Rhodes), she alludes to an ancient statue one hundred feet high. [Brackets]

3. Bartholdi was determined to build "A mighty woman—Mother of Exiles" and place her in New York Harbor. [Ellipsis mark]

4. He traveled all over America, to Boston, Chicago, Denver, Salt Lake City, and many other places, to promote his idea. [Dashes]

5. He was amazed at the country's size, industry, and enthusiasm for creating things, buildings, that is, not art. [Parentheses]

6. Bartholdi discovered that money, the enthusiasm of US citizens, and political support, all necessary for his project, were hard to get. [Parentheses]

7. He decided on a novel, hands-on approach, allowing people to climb into completed parts of the statue. [Dash]

8. Three cities were chosen: [1] In Philadelphia, the statue's hand and torch attracted Centennial Exhibition visitors; [2] in New York, the same exhibit drew people downtown; and [3] in Paris, visitors explored the statue's head and shoulders. [Parentheses]

9. When more money was needed, wealthy newspaper publisher Joseph Pulitzer, an immigrant himself, turned to nonwealthy Americans, working-class men, women, and children, and it was their small gifts that paid for the statue's pedestal. [Dashes]

10. Their gifts allowed Miss Liberty's torch to shine out over the water to say, "Send these, the homeless, tempest-tost to me, I lift my lamp beside the golden door." [Slash]

Van Goor and Hacker, *Developmental Exercises for*
The Bedford Handbook, 9th ed. (Boston: Bedford, 2014)

39-2 | Other punctuation marks **149**

EXERCISE 39-3 ◆ Other punctuation marks

To read about this topic, see section 39 in *The Bedford Handbook*, Ninth Edition.

The dashes, parentheses, brackets, ellipsis marks, and slashes in the following sentences are not well used. Edit the sentences to be more effective by deleting punctuation marks, replacing them with other marks, or restructuring the sentences. Refer to "The New Colossus" (p. 147) as necessary. Example:

> **On October 29, 1886 , ⫻ one hundred and ten years after the signing of the Declaration of**
>
> **Independence , ⫻ Miss Liberty was formally dedicated.**

1. Miss Liberty was the only woman at her dedication (except for two Frenchwomen who came with the sculptor).

2. On that day, the Lady whose "beacon hand/Glow(ed) world-wide welcome" was almost obscured from view by rain and wind.

3. Also, the crowds of people pushing and shoving resembled the ". . . huddled masses" Emma Lazarus wrote about.

4. The crowd—crushed together—trying to listen to the main speaker—he was William M. Evarts—could hear other voices too.

5. Women who were angry about being excluded from the ceremony had sailed in close to the island (they had chartered a boat) and were yelling their protests.

6. With all of the noise from the crowd and/or the women, the speaker paused.

7. He paused so long that an aide thought the speech was over. The aide signaled Bartholdi (who was waiting inside the statue).

8. Bartholdi saw the signal and unveiled the statue . . . an hour early.

9. The plaque with Emma Lazarus's poem on it was not on the statue at this time; it was added later—in 1903—without any special ceremony.

10. It is still there today for all visitors to read/ponder as they meet America's most beloved lady.

Van Goor and Hacker, *Developmental Exercises for The Bedford Handbook*, 9th ed. (Boston: Bedford, 2014)

EXERCISE 39-4 ◆ Other punctuation marks: Guided review

Edit the following paragraphs for the most effective use of the dash, parentheses, brackets, the ellipsis mark, and the slash. Refer to "The New Colossus" (p. 147) as necessary. The numbers in the margin refer to relevant rules in section 39 of *The Bedford Handbook*, Ninth Edition. The first revision has been done for you.

fourteen-line

The sonnet is a poem ~~/ of fourteen lines /~~ with a particular pattern to its   39a

rhymes; it is often used to compare or contrast two items. Emma Lazarus's poem "The

New Colossus" is a sonnet. Lazarus uses its fourteen lines to contrast two statues.

The ancient Colossus of Rhodes (which was male) represented the sun god; the new   39b

Colossus was female and represented liberty. The Rhodes Colossus symbolized what

Lazarus calls "storied pomp." The French-made American statue stood for freedom and

opportunity.

In her first line, "Not like the brazen (bronze) giant of Greek fame," Lazarus   39c

refers to the material of which the old Colossus was made. Bronze, a valuable metal

when the Colossus of Rhodes was erected in 280 BC, was available only to the wealthy.

Miss Liberty was made of copper, a material available to all classes of people. When

Miss Liberty was erected in 1898, America's least valuable coin—the one-cent piece,   39a

was made from copper. Miss Liberty was for everyone, not just the wealthy.

The major contrast Lazarus sets up is in the attitudes of the two statues. The

old Colossus is powerful, not caring about the ". . . wretched refuse" of its "teeming   39d

shore." The new one welcomes all: "Send these, the homeless, tempest-tost to me, I lift   39e

my lamp beside the golden door."

REVIEW OF 32–39 ◆ Punctuation

Edit the following paragraphs to correct errors in punctuation or to use more effective punctuation. Refer to the poem "The New Colossus" (p. 147) as necessary. The numbers in the margin refer to relevant rules in sections 32–39 of *The Bedford Handbook*, Ninth Edition. The first revision has been done for you.

The outside of the Statue of Liberty is made of copper, but what is inside the   32a

statue. Inside the statue are: iron braces and staircases. The thin copper plates that   38b, 35c

form the outside of the statue are bolted to a network of iron braces. There are several

staircases allowing workers and tourists to climb all the way into the head and the

torch. (This intricate network of braces and stairways was designed by Alexandre-

Gustave Eiffel; the same man who designed the famous Eiffel Tower in Paris.)   34d

For some years, the lighting equipment for Miss Libertys torch was also inside.   36a

Soon after the statue was set up for example engineers tried Edison's new invention,   32f

the electric lightbulb. They cut holes in the torch's copper sheets and hung lightbulbs

inside. Later, the copper sheets came down and glass windows went up. Giving Miss

Liberty a light that everyone would recognize as hers, challenged engineers and   33b

designers for sixty more years. When the statue was restored in the 1980s part of   32b

the lighting equipment was moved outside. Floodlights were installed on the torch's

balcony, and focused on thin gold sheets that form the torch ". . . whose flame / Is the   33a, 39d

imprisoned lightning. Miss Liberty will be able to welcome newcomers for many years.   37a

Van Goor and Hacker, *Developmental Exercises for*
The Bedford Handbook, 9th ed. (Boston: Bedford, 2014)

EXERCISE 40/41/42-1 ◆ Abbreviations, numbers, and italics: Guided practice

Correct any errors in abbreviations, numbers, and italics in the following paragraphs. The numbers in the margin refer to relevant rules in sections 40, 41, and 42 of *The Bedford Handbook*, Ninth Edition. The first revision has been done for you; a suggested revision of these paragraphs appears in the back of this book.

Everyone has heard of Christopher Columbus, but not many people know much
about him. Most people learn that he discovered America in ~~1492 AD.~~ *AD 1492.* Some people   40c
know that he had three ships, and they might be able to name them. (The ships were
the "Niña," the "Pinta," and the "Santa María.") A few people might even remember   42b
that Columbus thought he had found the Indies. And those with great self-confidence
might be willing to guess at the number of trips he made to his Indies. (It was 4.)   41a
Probably no one could tell you his favorite word, adelante.   42d

If they were asked what Columbus was trying to prove with his expensive
journey, most people would reply that he was trying to prove that the world is round.
They would be wrong. If they were asked what Columbus meant by the term Indies,   42d
they would probably say "India." They would be wrong again. If they were asked what
Columbus's rank was, they would most likely say "captain." They would be wrong
again. If they were asked what his sailors feared most, a no. of them would reply,   40e
"They feared that the boats would fall off the edge of the earth." And they would be
wrong again.

Isn't it strange that people can be so ignorant about a well-known man like
Columbus?

EXERCISE 40/41/42-2 ◆ Abbreviations and numbers

To read about this topic, see sections 40 and 41 in *The Bedford Handbook*, Ninth Edition.

 Edit the following sentences to correct errors in the use of abbreviations. Mark the one correct sentence "OK." Example:

> **The sailors who voyaged with Columbus used the same four directions sailors still use:**
> *north, south, east, and west.*
> ~~N, S, E, and W.~~
> ^

1. Sailors in AD 1492 knew the world was round; they were not afraid of sailing off the edge of the world.

2. They worried about more serious things—e.g., whether the wind would blow both ways so they could get back to Spain.

3. They also weren't sure about distances; however, one famous Italian prof., Dr. Toscanelli, thought he knew.

4. He was willing to estimate the distance from Lisbon, Port., to Japan.

5. He said that the exact no. of miles between the two places was three thousand nautical miles.

B Edit the following sentences to correct errors in the use of numbers. Mark the one correct sentence "OK." Example:

> *three*
> **Dr. Toscanelli set the distance at ~~3~~ thousand nautical miles.**
> ^

6. In twelve ninety-eight, Marco Polo wrote a book about his travels to the Indies.

7. 7,448 islands were in the Indies, according to Marco Polo's book.

8. Columbus was 41 when he convinced Queen Isabella to send him to find those islands.

9. As part of the contract, Columbus demanded ten % of the treasure he brought back to Spain.

10. At 8:00 a.m. on August 3, 1492, Columbus set out from Spain for the Indies.

Van Goor and Hacker, *Developmental Exercises for*
The Bedford Handbook, 9th ed. (Boston: Bedford, 2014)

EXERCISE 40/41/42-3 ◆ Italics

To read about this topic, see section 42 in *The Bedford Handbook*, Ninth Edition.

Edit the following sentences to correct the use of italics. Example:

Description of the World.
Marco Polo's book was titled ~~"Description of the World."~~
                                                                    ^

1. On the "Niña," the "Pinta," and the "Santa María," Columbus brought along one hundred men, all kinds of supplies, and enough cats to control the rat population.

2. Columbus always spoke the same word to his men—Adelante! (That means "Forward!" or "Sail on!")

3. Marco Polo's book had not prepared the men for seeing the same horizon week after week, seemingly ad infinitum.

4. To every fear or complaint, Columbus simply replied "Forward!" and that word forward began to get on the sailors' nerves.

5. Finally, Columbus's fleet made landfall on several groups of islands, some of which Columbus named after stories he had read in the *Bible* about King Solomon's travels and treasures.

Van Goor and Hacker, *Developmental Exercises for*
The Bedford Handbook, 9th ed. (Boston: Bedford, 2014)

40/41/42-3 | Italics **155**

EXERCISE 40/41/42-4 ◆ Abbreviations, numbers, and italics: Guided review

Correct any errors in the use of abbreviations, numbers, and italics in the following paragraphs. The numbers in the margin refer to relevant rules in sections 40, 41, and 42 of *The Bedford Handbook*, Ninth Edition. The first revision has been done for you.

Columbus's first voyage, in 1492, ~~AD,~~ was successful. Pleased with the gifts he 40c
had brought back and impressed by his reports, King Ferdinand and Queen Isabella
quickly ordered him to organize another voyage. Columbus was delighted to do so. At
first his luck held. Led by the flagship Maríagalante, a fleet of 17 ships and a thousand 42b, 41a
men who wanted to colonize the new land made the second trip in twenty-one days.
Columbus's good fortune, however, did not last. Life went downhill for the Italian
sailor from that time on.

The so-called Admiral of the Ocean Seas (a title Columbus had given himself)
had one disastrous experience after another. When he got back to the recently settled
town he had left, the whole settlement had been destroyed, and the 39 men he had left 41a
there were all dead. Columbus quickly found a new spot for his new colony, the first
European colony in America. The new site had serious drawbacks, e.g., bad water and 40e
many mosquitoes. Embarrassed, Columbus had to send Queen Isabella's ships back
for help; he loaded them not with gold but with pepper, sandalwood, and a no. of 40e
exotic birds.

Other voyages followed, but each turned out worse than the one before it. Not
even his favorite word, *adelante*, seemed to work for Columbus anymore. His first
voyage had definitely been the most successful.

Van Goor and Hacker, *Developmental Exercises for*
The Bedford Handbook, 9th ed. (Boston: Bedford, 2014)

Name _____ Section _____ Date _____

EXERCISE 43/44/45-1 ◆ Spelling, the hyphen, and capitalization: Guided practice

Edit the following paragraphs to correct misspellings and errors in the use of the hyphen and capitalization. The numbers in the margin refer to relevant rules in sections 43, 44, and 45 of *The Bedford Handbook*, Ninth Edition. The first revision has been done for you; a revision of these paragraphs appears in the back of this book.

Columbus's return to Spain from his first exploration was difficult. The *Niña*
and the *Pinta* were separated, the *Niña* almost sank, and the governor on the island
of Santa María had put Columbus's whole crew in jail. It seemed a miracle that both
boats survived ~~there~~ *their* journeys and arrived in the harbor at Palos on the same day.   43c

As difficult as that return was, the reception at court quite made up for it.
Columbus certainly made an all out effort to impress the court, the city, and the entire   44d
country. Lavishly attired, he recieved a grand welcome as he led his entourage into   43a
Barcelona, the spanish capital. It must have been a sight to behold: A procession like   45a, 45f
none Barcelona had ever seen before. Leading the parade was a gaudily-bedecked   44b
horse carrying Columbus, followed by six captive "indians" and all the crew. Everyone   45a
but Columbus was carrying boxes, baskets, and cages full of interesting and exotic
items.

When the group reached the throne room, King Ferdinand and Queen Isabella
stood up to greet Columbus formally and to admire his apron covered captives.   44b
Columbus asked the royal couple to except gifts of plants, shells, darts, thread, and   43c
gold. As intrigued as they were with the other gifts, King Ferdinand and Queen
Isabella basically wanted the gold. Luckily, Columbus had collected enough of it to
satisfy them.

By the end of his first week home, Columbus had such prestige that everyone
wanted to accomodate the wishes of the Italian sailor at the court of Spain. Columbus   43d
had no doubt that he would receive a Commission for a second voyage of exploration   45a
or even colonization.

EXERCISE 43/44/45-2 ◆ Spelling

To read about this topic, see section 43 in *The Bedford Handbook*, Ninth Edition.

Edit the following sentences to correct spelling errors. (Hint: There are ten errors.) Example:

> *incredibly*   *believed*
> **Others may have considered him ~~incredibally~~ lucky, but Columbus ~~beleived~~ he had been**
>   ^   ^
> **called by God to be the one to find a new sea route to the Indies.**

1. To begin with, he was born in Genoa, Italy, the best place concievable for someone who wanted to be in the sailing busness, since Genoa was a major seaport.

2. Other people said his being born there was all "just chance"; Columbus prefered to think that it was part of God's arrangment for him.

3. He was not suprised to be the sole survivor of a shipwreck that occured when he was twenty-five.

4. Weather others excepted the idea or not, Columbus knew he survived such a disasterous event because God had plans for him.

5. He thought that even his name emphasized his calling: *Christopher* means "Christ-bearing," and he would take Christ's name to the "heatherns" in India.

Van Goor and Hacker, *Developmental Exercises for The Bedford Handbook,* 9th ed. (Boston: Bedford, 2014)

EXERCISE 43/44/45-3 ◆ The hyphen

To read about this topic, see section 44 in *The Bedford Handbook*, Ninth Edition.

The writer of the following sentences got hyphen-happy. Remove six of the eleven hyphens. If a sentence needs no hyphens removed, mark it "OK." Example:

> **Columbus's all-consuming goal made him think that God͟himself had worked͟but the fortuitous marriage Columbus made in 1478.**

1. Marrying into a noble-family when he was thirty-three gave Columbus direct-access to the king of Portugal.

2. When the king firmly-declined Columbus's request to finance an exploratory-voyage, this well-known sailor decided he was supposed to go to Spain.

3. Queen Isabella was determined to make everyone into a practicing-Christian; because Columbus was religious, she did not consider the voyage a half-witted proposal.

4. After his discovery of "India," Columbus received confirmation of his self-given title, Admiral of the Ocean Seas and Viceroy of the Indies.

5. When the *Santa María* was wrecked, Columbus saw the incident as his God-given opportunity to go back posthaste to Spain, recruit more men, and return to this newly-found land.

Van Goor and Hacker, *Developmental Exercises for The Bedford Handbook,* 9th ed. (Boston: Bedford, 2014)

43/44/45-3 | The hyphen   **159**

EXERCISE 43/44/45-4 ◆ Capitalization

To read about this topic, see section 45 in *The Bedford Handbook*, Ninth Edition.

Edit the following paragraphs to correct errors in capitalization. The first sentence has been edited for you. You should find ten more errors.

      If Columbus had made his return trip first, he might not have been so eager to set out for

Indies.
the ~~indies.~~ The voyage turned out all right, but it had its bad times.

      To begin with, the *Niña* and the *Pinta* were separated on the way back to Spain. The

weather was very bad, especially when the two ships ran into a storm west of the Azores. The *Niña*

almost sank. Columbus was so sure it was going down that he put a record of his Discoveries in a

small barrel, sealed it completely, and threw it overboard. That way, if the ship went down, there

was still a chance that someone would learn of his discoveries. Actually, the ship made it to Santa

María, a portuguese island. The governor there thought Columbus was lying about his adventures

and arrested the crew. The crew was released only because Columbus threatened to shoot up

the town.

      The *Niña* was thrown off course again, but then Columbus's luck turned. The boat came

into Lisbon, and Columbus was a guest of king John II for a brief time before he took off for Spain

again. finally, the *Niña* made it home. On March 15, 1493, it sailed into the harbor at Palos. The

Pinta arrived shortly afterward on the same day. Such a coincidence certainly seemed to be a

sign of Divine approval and delighted Columbus. When queen Isabella saw what Columbus had

brought back, she was impressed. She thought that god had surely had a hand in the matter.

Certainly many influences had played a part in his success that Spring. Even Marco Polo's book

Description of the world had played a role: Getting Columbus started on the journey. Columbus

was convinced that his life was just one miracle after another. "I've been chosen," he might have

said. "God has chosen me."

Van Goor and Hacker, *Developmental Exercises for*
The Bedford Handbook, 9th ed. (Boston: Bedford, 2014)

EXERCISE 43/44/45-5 ◆ Spelling, the hyphen, and capitalization: Guided review

Correct any errors in spelling or in the use of the hyphen or capitalization in the following paragraphs. The numbers in the margin refer to relevant rules in sections 43, 44, and 45 of *The Bedford Handbook*, Ninth Edition. The first revision has been done for you.

After being feted, feasted, and honored on his return from his first voyage across

the ocean, Columbus must have told and ~~re told~~ *retold* the story of his trip. He would have   44a

told listeners how, after the ships had sailed for twenty one days, his men threatened   44c

to turn back because they had never sailed so far west before. Columbus, sure of

his special calling as an explorer, promised them that they would sight land within

three days. On the evening of the third day, at ten o'clock, he thought he saw a light

and alerted a nearby servant. Both of them lost sight of it almost at once. But at two

o'clock the next morning, a cannon shot sounded from the *Pinta*. "Land! Land!" cried

the sailors. Columbus had kept his promise. No wonder he began to sign his name

with a secret code to show that he was more special then other people.   43c

Retelling the story of his voyage, Columbus would have described the beautiful

Island that the ships first landed on. He named it San Salvador. He would have told   45a

how, at every island he and his men visited, natives had flocked to the boats to see the

strangers. One day, more than a thousand people had come in just one hour. Columbus

had spent three months exploring and setting up a fort before leaving for the return

trip to Spain. And on their return, eight months later, he and his crew had recieved a   43a

royal welcome.

Yes, he had had a few problems on the trip out, and the return trip had been

very hard, but one set of memories was indelibly imprinted on Columbus's brain: The   45f

memories of that remarkably successful first voyage.

REVIEW OF 40–45 ◆ Mechanics

This essay has eleven errors in spelling and mechanics. The numbers in the margin refer to relevant rules in sections 40–45 of *The Bedford Handbook*, Ninth Edition. The first correction has been made for you. Find and correct ten more errors.

Columbus made an all-out effort to find the Indies—India, China, the East   44d

Indies, and Japan. Instead, he found Cuba, Venezuela, the Bahamas, and the Coasts   45a

of South and Central America. Unable to find gold, he captured 500 natives and had   41a

them shipped back to Spain to be sold as slaves. He punished the natives so severely

when they did not bring him gold that in two years one third of them ran away or   44c

were killed or sold. Things went from bad to worse; e.g., many settlers died of illness,   40d

and some went back to Spain with bad reports of Columbus's governance. Convinced

that God was unhappy with him for some transgression, Columbus returned to Spain

wearing a monk's course garb and walking humbly. People gave him a new title: 43c

Columbus, Admiral of the Mosquitoes.

Ferdinand and Isabella gave him another opportunity, though, and on May

thirtieth, 1498, Columbus set out again. The voyage was disasterous, with Columbus   41b, 43d

ending up back in Spain, this time in chains. Columbus got one more chance, but

hurricanes and storms plagued him. He wrote, "other tempests have I seen, but none   45e

so long or so grim as this." He must by now have realized that Dr. Toscanelli did not no   43c

his geography very well. Yet "Sail on!" was still his answer to every setback.

When Columbus got back to Spain, sick and exhausted, queen Isabella died   45b

before he could see her. Columbus himself died still insisting he had found the Indies.

He had not, of course. He had done far more: He had discovered a "new world."

Van Goor and Hacker, *Developmental Exercises for The Bedford Handbook,* 9th ed. (Boston: Bedford, 2014)

EXERCISE 46-1 ◆ Parts of speech: Preview

To read about this topic, see section 46 in *The Bedford Handbook*, Ninth Edition.

In the following paragraphs, label the part of speech of each italicized word. Use these codes: noun (N), pronoun (PN), helping verb (HV), main verb (MV), adjective (ADJ), adverb (ADV), preposition (P), conjunction (C). The first word has been labeled for you; answers to this exercise appear in the back of this book.

                                                   MV

America's Declaration of Independence *seems* very formal to today's *readers*. Many of its sentences *are* long and involved, and some *of* its words seem old-fashioned. But *its* central message is loud *and* clear to all those who take the time to read and understand it, whether they are schoolchildren *or* adult immigrants.

Those somewhat *formal* words contain both a declaration and a promise. The Declaration *starts* with a seventy-one-word statement called the "Preamble." It *simply* says that when one group of people break their ties *with* another, those people *should* tell *everyone* their reasons for breaking up.

In the next part, called the "Declaration of Rights," the colonists list their basic assumptions *about* life—that everyone is born with *certain* rights ("life, liberty, and the pursuit of happiness"); that governments have power only *when* people give it to *them*; and that when a government repeatedly *acts* in ways that deny people's rights, people have a right and a duty to overthrow that *government* and build another one.

It was a *bold* beginning for a bold document—a declaration promising freedom that has *been* celebrated by Americans for more than two hundred years.

Van Goor and Hacker, *Developmental Exercises for The Bedford Handbook*, 9th ed. (Boston: Bedford, 2014)

46-1 | Parts of speech: Preview **163**

EXERCISE 46-2 ◆ Nouns and noun/adjectives

To read about this topic, see section 46a in *The Bedford Handbook*, Ninth Edition.

A Each of the following groups of three words contains only one noun. Circle the noun. Example:

| national | nationwide | (nation) |

1. defendable	defend	defenses
2. speaking	speaker	speak
3. just	justice	justly
4. normal	normally	normality
5. repetition	repeating	repeated

B Underline each noun (including noun/adjectives) in the following sentences. Examples:

When they apply for American citizenship, refugee immigrants must study some famous

American documents.

6. Schoolchildren and new citizens have similar homework assignments.

7. They both must learn the Pledge of Allegiance to the country's flag.

8. Many of these people also memorize the opening words of the Declaration of Independence.

9. The Preamble to the Constitution is often assigned, as well as some famous speeches and the national anthem.

10. If students pass their tests on all of this, they are promoted; if immigrants pass theirs, they are welcomed into American citizenship.

Van Goor and Hacker, *Developmental Exercises for The Bedford Handbook*, 9th ed. (Boston: Bedford, 2014)

EXERCISE 46-3 ◆ Nouns and noun/adjectives

To read about this topic, see section 46a in *The Bedford Handbook*, Ninth Edition.

All of the following paired sentences contain some form of the word *exhibit*. In each pair, circle the letter of the sentence that uses the word *exhibit* as a noun or noun/adjective; be prepared to explain how you know it is a noun. (Hint: There is only one noun/adjective.) Example:

a. The Declaration of Independence is on exhibit at the National Archives in Washington, DC.

b. The Archives exhibits the Declaration of Independence for many tourist groups.

1. a. Many people do not realize that the exhibits in the national museums change frequently.

   b. Each museum exhibits a wide variety of materials.

2. a. Museums can exhibit something of interest to almost any visitor.

   b. It is impossible to predict which exhibit any one visitor will enjoy.

3. a. Most children prefer an interactive exhibit over any other kind.

   b. The children can exhibit their own skill in operating the interactive devices.

4. a. Most of the exhibit halls have excellent signs and explanations about what the visitor can see.

   b. Curators can exhibit rare items safely in specially constructed cases.

5. a. When the museums are exhibiting items borrowed from another place, visitors have a limited time to visit the displays.

   b. When exhibits contain items from other collections, however, many more people can see and enjoy those items.

Van Goor and Hacker, *Developmental Exercises for The Bedford Handbook*, 9th ed. (Boston: Bedford, 2014)

46-3 | Nouns and noun/adjectives **165**

EXERCISE 46-4 ◆ Pronouns and pronoun/adjectives

To read about this topic, see section 46b in *The Bedford Handbook*, Ninth Edition.

A Circle the five pronouns in each group of six words. Example:

(his)　(they)　under　(whoever)　(no one)　(themselves)

1.	I	she	of	he	ours	everyone
2.	her	me	it	to	whose	many
3.	for	him	you	us	this	someone
4.	they	my	that	we	from	some
5.	in	them	mine	your	these	nothing
6.	at	yours	her	his	all	none
7.	hers	our	its	nobody	another	over
8.	under	myself	their	yours	each	several
9.	from	theirs	who	which	either	something
10.	whom	those	any	both	few	through

B Underline the pronouns (including pronoun/adjectives) in the following sentences. Except in the example, there are two in each sentence. Example:

Our Declaration of Independence includes these famous words: "We hold these truths to be self-evident."

11. Whoever reads the Declaration of Independence finds a message for everyone.

12. One of its basic premises is the equality of people.

13. Furthermore, the Declaration declares, "They are endowed by their Creator with certain unalienable rights."

14. "Among these are life, liberty, and the pursuit of happiness" may be its most famous line.

15. Refugees who apply for citizenship are claiming those rights.

Van Goor and Hacker, *Developmental Exercises for The Bedford Handbook,* 9th ed. (Boston: Bedford, 2014)

EXERCISE 46-5 ◆ Verbs

To read about this topic, see section 46c in *The Bedford Handbook*, Ninth Edition.

A All of the following paired sentences contain some form of the word *promise*. In each pair, circle the letter of the sentence that uses a form of the word *promise* as a verb. (Hint: The words *promised* and *promising* can sometimes function as adjectives.) Example:

    a.   The founders of this country made certain promises to one another.

    (b.) Each document of this country promises special things to the people who live here.

1. a.   In a way, the Constitution is a set of promises.

     b.   The government promises to do certain things for citizens.

2. a.   In turn, the citizens must promise to obey certain laws.

     b.   The citizens' promise is just as important as the government's.

3. a.   Some early citizens thought the Constitution had not promised them enough rights.

     b.   They thought that the promised rights were not specific enough.

4. a.   By adding a Bill of Rights to the Constitution, citizens demanded a promise about freedom of religion.

     b.   The Bill of Rights does indeed promise freedom of religion.

5. a.   One of the most promising signs of political health in the colonies was their insistence on gaining certain rights.

     b.   Whenever citizens repeat their oath of allegiance, they are promising anew to honor the Constitution.

B Underline all verbs in the following paragraph and label them MV (main verb) or HV (helping verb). The first sentence has been done for you.

               HV MV

Who <u>should</u> <u>vote</u>? All citizens should go to the polls and vote. When citizens do this, they are

making important choices that can affect their lives and the lives of others. In addition, citizens

must tell their elected representatives how they feel about certain issues. If the representatives

ignore these messages, they may lose their jobs. It is important that these representatives stay in

touch with the voters, but it is just as important that the voters send messages. Without this kind

of communication, America's great democratic experiment will fail.

EXERCISE 46-6 ◆ Adjectives and adverbs

To read about this topic, see sections 46d and 46e in *The Bedford Handbook*, Ninth Edition.

A | Label each of the following words as an adjective (ADJ) or an adverb (ADV). You should find twelve adjectives and eight adverbs. Example:

clean ___ADJ___

1. inexpensive _____
2. very _____
3. rude _____
4. not _____
5. crazy _____
6. lovely _____
7. extremely _____

8. beautiful _____
9. sometimes _____
10. political _____
11. ten _____
12. never _____
13. tired _____
14. aloud _____

15. rich _____
16. lonely _____
17. oily _____
18. slowly _____
19. always _____
20. common _____

B | Label the adjectives (ADJ) and adverbs (ADV) in the following sentences. Ignore the articles *a*, *an*, and *the*. You should find ten adjectives and five adverbs. Example:

                                              ADJ   ADV   ADJ

The Constitution and the Bill of Rights are separate, but they go together as a single

document.

21. The Bill of Rights consists of the ten amendments that immediately follow the Constitution.

22. The First Amendment is the most familiar of the famous rights.

23. It guarantees religious freedom and freedom of speech for American citizens.

24. It also guarantees freedom of the press, an extremely important freedom in a democratic country.

25. Because representatives to the original Congress valued the right to discuss legislation publicly, the Bill of Rights assures citizens of the right to hold meetings and to petition the federal government.

Van Goor and Hacker, *Developmental Exercises for The Bedford Handbook*, 9th ed. (Boston: Bedford, 2014)

EXERCISE 46-7 ◆ Prepositions

To read about this topic, see section 46f in *The Bedford Handbook*, Ninth Edition.

A | Many prepositions express opposite ideas. Fill in the following blanks with prepositions that express the opposite idea to the one listed. Examples:

like ___unlike___   into ___out of___

1. above _____   6. after _____

2. against _____   7. down _____

3. in _____   8. inside _____

4. on _____   9. over _____

5. to _____   10. with _____

B | Circle all twenty prepositions in the following paragraph.

The men who wrote the Declaration of Independence dealt with many political controversies. In addition, they disagreed about many ideas. During their discussions, some felt they should come to terms with England, some wanted to give all of the reasons for their break with England, and some were against war under the existing circumstances. They argued over these issues frequently, making agreement seem impossible at first. They stuck to their task despite many disagreements among individuals, and in the end they put their thoughts into words that have remained famous to future generations.

Van Goor and Hacker, *Developmental Exercises for The Bedford Handbook,* 9th ed. (Boston: Bedford, 2014)

46-7 | Prepositions **169**

EXERCISE 46-8 ◆ Prepositions and conjunctions

To read about this topic, see sections 46f and 46g in *The Bedford Handbook*, Ninth Edition.

In the following sentences, label all prepositions (P), coordinating conjunctions (CC), and subordinating conjunctions (SUB). The numbers in the brackets after each sentence indicate how many of each you should find. Example:

> SUB   P   P   CC
> **When the Bill of Rights was adopted, it gave to American citizens rights and guarantees**
>   P   CC
> **none of the colonists or their predecessors had enjoyed. [3P, 2CC, 1SUB]**

1. When the founders of the United States wrote the Bill of Rights, they were recalling their past troubles with England. [3P, 1SUB]

2. They were also hoping that this new country and its laws would be different. [1CC, 1SUB]

3. Before the American Revolution, English officers and their men had been quartered in colonists' homes. [2P, 1CC]

4. The colonists often objected, but they could do nothing about the situation. [1P, 1CC]

5. Although they petitioned and appealed, nothing changed. [1CC, 1SUB]

6. Because the colonists objected to this practice, they put a special amendment about it in the Bill of Rights. [4P, 1SUB]

7. That amendment says that the government cannot make people give free room and board to soldiers unless the country is at war. [2P, 1CC, 2SUB]

8. Another problem was that, although the colonists objected, under English rule they and their homes could be searched by any magistrate or his appointees. [2P, 2CC, 2SUB]

9. Another amendment to the Bill of Rights would protect citizens from unreasonable searches; searching a citizen's home would require a warrant. [3P]

10. Because the Bill of Rights was added to the Constitution, Americans are still protected from these and several other intrusions by the government. [4P, 1CC, 1SUB]

Van Goor and Hacker, *Developmental Exercises for The Bedford Handbook*, 9th ed. (Boston: Bedford, 2014)

EXERCISE 46-9 ◆ Parts of speech: Review

To read about this topic, see section 46 in *The Bedford Handbook*, Ninth Edition.

In the following paragraphs, label the parts of speech of the italicized words using these codes: noun (N), pronoun (PN), helping verb (HV), main verb (MV), adjective (ADJ), adverb (ADV), preposition (P), conjunction (C). The first word has been labeled for you.

                  ADJ

Americans fought a long *hard* war to secure the freedoms and rights that *their* Declaration proclaimed. Even *while* the war was going on, France (America's ally) *was* trying to get America to agree *to* a truce. France proposed a treaty that *would* give America its independence *without* any questions. But under the French *proposal*, the boundaries of America would be established *by* which country's army was *currently* in control of the land. That would give Spain *and* France control of major portions *of* the land Americans claimed. John Adams, America's *negotiator*, refused to discuss such a plan.

    Adams was simply carrying out the spirit of the Declaration that had started the war. In the final *section* of their Declaration of Independence, the Americans had *used* another impossibly long sentence—more than one hundred words—to declare their separation from Great Britain and their determination to make their own decisions. They could *not* have known then how *costly* defending that Declaration would be. *But* when the war was over, the colonists had won the rights for which *they* had pledged their lives, their fortunes, and their *sacred* honor.

EXERCISE 47-1 ◆ Sentence patterns: Preview

To read about this topic, see section 47 in *The Bedford Handbook*, Ninth Edition.

Label the function of each italicized word or word group in the following paragraphs. Use these codes: subject (S), verb (V), subject complement (SC), direct object (DO), indirect object (IO), and object complement (OC). The first sentence has been labeled for you; answers to this exercise appear in the back of this book.

New art *forms* often *lead* the *public* to a new way of looking at things. Frequently, however, viewers are not yet ready to understand the new forms.

A *group* of French artists *had* this *problem* in the 1800s. These artists completely changed their way of painting. Instead of painting in the subdued, dark tones of a formal studio, *they* often *went* outdoors. One of their new techniques was the use of color. *They* nearly always *gave* their *paintings* great *bursts* of color, like sunlight on a field. Art *lovers* in France *were surprised* by such bright colors on the artists' canvases. People often called such paintings "open-air paintings." These *artists* usually *made* even their indoor *scenes* very *bright* with light and colors. Through an open window onto a bouquet of flowers or a bright-haired child *would pour* bright *sunshine*. *Were* Pierre-Auguste Renoir's *paintings* always *bright* and *cheerful*? Yes, and those of Claude Monet, Camille Pissarro, and Paul Cézanne were equally pleasant. These *painters*, now called "impressionists," *are admired* all over the world today, but in their own time the artists had to educate their viewers.

Twentieth-century artists had the same problem. Two new art *forms* from that period *are* good *examples*, "op art" and "pop art." *Both* of these *showed* their *viewers* everyday *objects* in quite different ways. Both eventually attracted a following. But like many artists before them, the op-art and pop-art painters had to educate their viewers first.

Van Goor and Hacker, *Developmental Exercises for The Bedford Handbook*, 9th ed. (Boston: Bedford, 2014)

EXERCISE 47-2 ◆ Subjects

To read about this topic, see section 47 in *The Bedford Handbook*, Ninth Edition.

A Each of the following sentences has three words or word groups italicized. One of these words or word groups is the subject. Find it and label it S. Example:

        S

Many *artists* have *preferred* certain colors for their *work*.

1. During one *part* of his life, *Picasso* preferred the color *blue*.

2. *There* are many famous *paintings* by Picasso from *this* period.

3. "*Blue*" refers not only to the predominant *color* of these paintings but also to their *mood*.

4. In these paintings *you* will find *outcasts* or victims of *society* as the main characters.

5. Do the *derelicts and beggars* in these pictures reflect *Picasso's* own sense of *isolation*?

B In the following paragraph, complete subjects have been italicized. Label the simple subject (or subjects) SS. The first sentence has been labeled for you.

        SS   SS

Pierre-Auguste Renoir and his young friends founded a new movement called "impressionism."
Instead of trying to reproduce a scene exactly, *impressionist painters like Renoir and his friends*
blended small brushstrokes of different colors to give a general impression of a scene. Up close,
a careful observer of a restaurant scene sees no solid edges on a table or a lady's hat, just small
dabs of paint. At a distance, however, *that same careful observer* will clearly see the picture in the
artist's mind. At first *the art world* laughed at and rejected the new movement. However, there is
now *no serious argument about the importance of the impressionist movement*.

Van Goor and Hacker, *Developmental Exercises for*
The Bedford Handbook, 9th ed. (Boston: Bedford, 2014)

47-2 | Subjects   **173**

EXERCISE 47-3 ◆ Direct objects and subject complements

To read about this topic, see section 47b in *The Bedford Handbook*, Ninth Edition.

A Subjects and verbs have been labeled in the following sentences. Label each italicized word as a simple direct object (DO) or a simple subject complement (SC). Example:

                         S   V   SC

Pierre-Auguste Renoir's parents were *supportive* of their son's ambitions.

              S   V

1. Renoir's love of art was *clear* to his parents.

           S V   S   V

2. When he was a *boy* of thirteen, they apprenticed *him* to a porcelain artist.

          S   V

3. Renoir first learned the potter's *trade*.

          S   V

4. Soon he was quite *skillful* at making and firing vases.

          S   V

5. He enjoyed the *task* of decorating the vases even more.

B Using the pattern of each sentence as a model, write a short sentence of your own on any subject. Example:

S/V/SC: Renoir was an artist.

Casey was a ballplayer. _____

6. S/V: Renoir studied.

_____

7. S/V: Renoir studied hard.

_____

8. S/V/SC: He became an excellent painter.

_____

9. S/V/SC: His paintings are cheerful.

_____

10. S/V/DO: Café owners liked his murals.

_____

Van Goor and Hacker, *Developmental Exercises for The Bedford Handbook*, 9th ed. (Boston: Bedford, 2014)

EXERCISE 47-4 ◆ Indirect objects and object complements

To read about this topic, see section 47b in *The Bedford Handbook*, Ninth Edition.

A Subjects, verbs, and direct objects are labeled in the following sentences. Label each italicized word as a simple indirect object (IO) or a simple object complement (OC). Example:

>   S   V   *IO*   DO
> **Renoir's parents gave *him* a good start in his chosen profession.**

1. Besides his parents, other people considered the young Renoir a fine *painter*.

2. He had shown local *businessmen* some of his work.

3. Owners of some Paris cafés gave *him* painting jobs.

4. He made the walls of their cafés *beautiful*.

5. The lovely scenes made both customers and owners *happy*.

B Using the pattern of each sentence as a model, write a short sentence of your own on any subject. Example:

S/V/DO/OC: Renoir called his style of painting "impressionist."

Casey called his style of batting "the best."

6. S/V/IO/DO: Paris café owners offered Renoir much work.

_____

7. S/V/IO/DO: They gave him twenty orders for murals.

_____

8. S/V/DO/OC: They considered his work exceptional.

_____

9. S/V/DO/OC: People called him "the happy painter."

_____

10. S/V: His popularity increased.

_____

EXERCISE 47-5 ◆ Direct objects, indirect objects, and object complements

To read about this topic, see section 47b in *The Bedford Handbook*, Ninth Edition.

Underline the verb of each sentence. Then label the complete direct object (DO) and any complete indirect objects (IO) or object complements (OC). Example:

> ┌─DO─┐   ┌──────DO──────┐ ┌──────OC──────┐
> **Many people <u>enjoy</u> pop art. They <u>find</u> this new kind of art a refreshing change.**

1. During World War II, American mass media flooded London.

2. The effect of that flood fascinated many London artists.

3. Using the American material, British artists gave the world a new art form.

4. To produce their art, the artists used images from popular culture.

5. Someone named the new art "pop art."

6. Most Americans find pop art very appealing.

7. To some, it reflects the optimism of the 1960s.

8. Items like flags, signs, and comic strips gave pop artists their subject matter.

9. Artists like Jasper Johns and Roy Lichtenstein preceded the more famous Andy Warhol.

10. Of all these artists, Andy Warhol best understood the media's power to affect people's thinking.

Van Goor and Hacker, *Developmental Exercises for The Bedford Handbook*, 9th ed. (Boston: Bedford, 2014)

EXERCISE 47-6 ◆ Sentence patterns: Review

To read about this topic, see section 47 in *The Bedford Handbook*, Ninth Edition.

Label the function of each italicized word or word group in the following paragraph using these codes: subject (S), verb (V), subject complement (SC), direct object (DO), indirect object (IO), and object complement (OC). The first sentence has been labeled for you.

        S   V   DO

    Renoir definitely *had* firm *ideas* about work and about getting along with people. As for work, he believed that *people* everywhere *should use* their *hands* every day. He certainly did, and because he did, *friends* often *called* this hardworking *man* a *workman-painter*. Being called a workman-painter pleased Renoir. Work seemed to be more important to him than the finished product. "The only *reward* for work *is* the *work* itself," he said. He got along with people very well; even his enemies seemed to like him. When his opponents attacked his views, *he* frequently *responded* by suggesting a compromise. *He* freely *offered* other *people* his own successful *techniques* for getting along with his opponents. According to Renoir, *you* certainly *should give* your *enemies* a *chance*. You should also avoid a fight whenever possible. Why? If you avoid fights, your *enemies* often *will become* your *friends*. The *joy* in Renoir's paintings *might be explained* by these approaches to life.

Van Goor and Hacker, *Developmental Exercises for The Bedford Handbook*, 9th ed. (Boston: Bedford, 2014)

47-6 | Sentence patterns: Review   **177**

EXERCISE 48-1 ◆ Subordinate word groups: Preview

To read about this topic, see section 48 in *The Bedford Handbook*, Ninth Edition.

In the following paragraphs, underline prepositional and verbal phrases once; underline subordinate clauses twice. One answer has been done for you; you should find thirteen more prepositional phrases, three verbal phrases, and four subordinate clauses. Answers to this exercise appear in the back of the book.

Parisian David Guetta, who has been called the lord of modern club music, also was responsible for bringing the music to American audiences. Guetta popularized club music—or house music—in Paris in the 1980s, when he worked as a DJ. He also released the album *Nation Rap*, which was a hip-hop collaboration with French rapper Sidney Duteil.

The club music phenomenon soon spread through Europe and the United States. American artists like Madonna, seeing the rise in popularity, began to incorporate house elements in their songs. Today house music is the center of massive music festivals like Miami's Winter Music Conference, which in 2012 had more than 200,000 attendees.

Van Goor and Hacker, *Developmental Exercises for The Bedford Handbook*, 9th ed. (Boston: Bedford, 2014)

EXERCISE 48-2 ◆ Prepositional phrases

To read about this topic, see section 48a in *The Bedford Handbook*, Ninth Edition.

Underline the twenty prepositional phrases in the following sentences. Example:

Early house music was generally dance-based, characterized <u>by repetitive four-four beats.</u>

1. Rhythms in the music centered around drum machines, off-beat cymbals, and synthesized bass.

2. House music displayed several characteristics of disco music of the seventies, but it was more electronic and minimalist.

3. Often the music's focus around a repetitive rhythm was more important than the lyrics or the melody.

4. House music today, maintaining several of these core elements, varies in style and influence.

5. If one artist has personified and largely been responsible for the widespread hysteria over dance club music, it's Parisian David Guetta.

6. His hits, such as "Without You" and "Club Can't Handle Me," sell millions and are known worldwide, and they are characterized by a blend of what he calls electro music and urban soul.

7. He is known for his easygoing, have-fun attitude, claiming that he produces his best music while he's having fun.

8. Though he is a soft-spoken man, he stays well connected with his fans; by 2012, he had thirty-one million followers on Facebook and four million on Twitter.

9. According to Guetta, what was once underground music is now just as formulaic as mainstream pop music played on the radio.

10. He is trying to do something new and completely outside the box.

Van Goor and Hacker, *Developmental Exercises for*
The Bedford Handbook, 9th ed. (Boston: Bedford, 2014)

48-2 | Prepositional phrases   **179**

EXERCISE 48-3 ◆ Prepositional and verbal phrases

To read about this topic, see sections 48a and 48b in *The Bedford Handbook*, Ninth Edition.

Some of the phrases in the following paragraphs are italicized. Label these phrases prepositional (PR), gerund (G), infinitive (I), or participial (PT). The first one has been labeled for you.

PR
David Guetta's career took off *in the early nineties* when he met American singer Robert Owens, who was touring in Europe, and played him one *of his own mixes*. Guetta asked Owens *to sing the vocals*, and the track was released in 1994 as "Up & Away." Known as Guetta's first single, this track is one of the pioneering recordings of French house music. While he was working as a DJ, Guetta and his wife, Cathy, threw parties, *called "Scream" parties*, and he also held events in Ibiza, Spain, *hosting a weekly dance party that has become famous worldwide*. *Impressed by the spectacle*, one music magazine called these Ibiza events "probably the most celebrated dance party *in the world*." Guests have included American television stars, rappers like Dr. Dre, and fashion designer Jean Paul Gaultier.

Over the past ten years or more, Guetta has become a master at working a room into a frenzy. As a DJ, he innovates by *remixing records live* and *slamming tracks together that no one else would pair*. *To maintain such energy* may seem impossible and is certainly impressive to his devotees, who find his live performances and parties unforgettable.

Van Goor and Hacker, *Developmental Exercises for The Bedford Handbook*, 9th ed. (Boston: Bedford, 2014)

EXERCISE 48-4 ◆ Verbal phrases

To read about this topic, see section 48b in *The Bedford Handbook*, Ninth Edition.

The verbal phrase in each of the following sentences has been italicized. Label these phrases gerund (G), participial (PT), or infinitive (I). Example:

> PT
> ***Making his debut as a producer,*** **David Guetta released "Just a Little More Love" in 2001.**

1. American gospel singer Chris Willis enjoyed *vacationing in France,* where he met Guetta and soon after recorded the vocal on the single.

2. The hit became an electro sensation, *popping up on club lists for years.*

3. *To experiment further,* Guetta made a bootleg remix of David Bowie's "Heroes," retitled "Just for One Day."

4. *Getting the go-ahead from Bowie* wasn't a problem, and Guetta officially released the track.

5. The single "Love Takes Over" was another smash hit *highlighting Kelly Rowland's soaring vocals.*

6. *Connecting with his audience* is always Guetta's primary motivation.

7. Guetta says the most important goal of being a DJ is *to make people feel good.*

8. *To be matter-of-fact about his success* is part of his personality, though he never comes across as boastful.

9. *Debunking the idea that the French are arrogant,* Guetta says, "They are just telling the truth."

10. When he contemplates his rise to fame, he says it is impossible not *to marvel at how the son of a Jewish-Moroccan sociology professor found such opportunity.*

Van Goor and Hacker, *Developmental Exercises for*
The Bedford Handbook, 9th ed. (Boston: Bedford, 2014)

48-4 | Verbal phrases   **181**

EXERCISE 48-5 ◆ Subordinate clauses

To read about this topic, see section 48e in *The Bedford Handbook*, Ninth Edition.

A Underline the subordinate clauses in the following sentences. Example:

When he was interviewed after winning a Grammy in 2011</u>, Guetta talked about future collaborations.

1. Guetta, who was late to the 2011 awards ceremony, wasn't able to collect the Grammy himself.

2. His shuffling, boyish manner makes it hard to believe that he is a genius with sound.

3. Because he is so upbeat, he is an easy target for sarcastic treatment and ridicule by the press.

4. Guetta shrugs off such put-downs as silly, even funny; his attitude shows that he does not lack a sense of humor about himself.

5. Even though he is a superstar, he does not look like one with his shaggy hair and simple clothes.

B Identify each of the following word groups as a prepositional phrase or a subordinate clause. Example:

    a. **As dance music spread**   *subordinate clause*

    b. **As a young DJ**   *prepositional phrase*

6. a. Before the show _____

   b. Before he had started the show _____

7. a. After he was presented with the award _____

   b. After the award presentation _____

8. a. Until his first big hit _____

   b. Until he had his first big hit _____

9. a. Since the dance music craze _____

   b. Since dance music became popular _____

10. a. As Guetta worked to change the industry _____

   b. As an industry pioneer _____

Van Goor and Hacker, *Developmental Exercises for The Bedford Handbook*, 9th ed. (Boston: Bedford, 2014)

EXERCISE 48-6 ◆ Subordinate word groups: Review

To read about this topic, see section 48 in *The Bedford Handbook*, Ninth Edition.

In the following paragraphs, underline prepositional and verbal phrases once; underline subordinate clauses twice. The first phrase has been underlined for you; you should find twenty more subordinate word groups.

David Guetta has built a phenomenal recording career. His recording pursuits started <u>in 2001</u>, when Guetta and Joachim Garraud founded Gum Productions and released the hit single "Just a Little More Love." They released the album of the same name the next year.

In 2004, Guetta's second album, *Guetta Blaster*, which contained the hit "The World Is Mine," was released. In 2007 came Guetta's third album, *Pop Life*. It was a hit in the UK and Ireland as well as in continental Europe. The lead single, "Love Is Gone," reached the top of the American dance chart, landing on the *Billboard* Hot 100.

Guetta's career is still rising; he won the 2011 Grammy Award for Best Remixed Recording for the song "Revolver," featuring Madonna. In 2012, Guetta was nominated for the Grammys for Best Dance Recording and Best Dance/Electronica Album. To add to his busy life, Guetta started his own label, Jack Back Records, which features only electronic music. His innovations with sound know no limit.

Van Goor and Hacker, *Developmental Exercises for
The Bedford Handbook*, 9th ed. (Boston: Bedford, 2014)

48-6 | Subordinate word groups: Review   **183**

EXERCISE 49-1 ◆ Sentence types: Preview

To read about this topic, see section 49 in *The Bedford Handbook*, Ninth Edition.

In the following paragraphs, indicate on the blank space after each sentence whether the sentence is simple (S), compound (C), complex (CX), or compound-complex (CC). Two blanks have been filled for you; answers to this exercise appear in the back of this book.

Most Americans of any age recognize the name Jackie Robinson. _____ Even if they are not sports fans, Americans know some basic facts about him. _____ Jackie Robinson played baseball, he was good at it, and he was the first black man on a major league team. ___C___ Even more important than what Jackie Robinson did on the ball field is what he did off the field. _____

Several off-the-field incidents occurred when he was in the army during World War II. ___CX___ His sports prowess was well known, and he was avidly recruited for both football and baseball teams. _____ Because the football team was not integrated, Robinson refused to play on any army team. _____ While he was still in the army—and a second lieutenant to boot—the driver of the bus taking soldiers from the base into town ordered Robinson to go to the back of the bus. _____ (In those days in the southern states, the front and middle sections of a bus were for whites only.) _____ Robinson knew his rights as a soldier; when he refused to go to the back, he was arrested. _____ When his case came up, Robinson defended himself in the military court and won. _____

These off-the-field incidents foreshadowed important events that followed. _____

Van Goor and Hacker, *Developmental Exercises for*
The Bedford Handbook, 9th ed. (Boston: Bedford, 2014)

EXERCISE 49-2 ◆ Sentence types

To read about this topic, see section 49 in *The Bedford Handbook*, Ninth Edition.

In the following sentences, underline any subordinate clauses. Then determine the sentence type and indicate it in the blank: simple, compound, complex, or compound-complex. (Hint: Some sentences do not have a subordinate clause.) Example:

In 1945, Branch Rickey was president and general manager of the Brooklyn Dodgers.

_simple_____

1. Driven by his ambition to build America's strongest baseball team, Rickey wanted the best talent in the world. _____

2. Believing also that keeping nonwhites out of baseball was morally wrong, he had been studying the players in the Negro leagues. _____

3. He needed someone who was as good off the field as on the field. _____

4. The Negro leagues had plenty of good players, and Rickey's scouts watched them all, reporting on each one. _____

5. Impressed by the reports on Robinson's family life and by his postponement of marriage until he had a job, Rickey wanted to meet this ballplayer. _____

6. Reports also showed Robinson's fiery temper; worried, Rickey flew Robinson to New York for an interview. _____

7. In the interview, Rickey taunted Robinson with snide remarks and mean insults, making it quite clear that Robinson's ability to deal with such things—on and off the field—was as important as his ability to play ball. _____

8. Robinson understood: He could not lose his temper on the field or off, he could not respond in kind even if he was physically attacked, and he had to maintain this nonviolent stance for at least three years. _____

9. It was not a role that Robinson was used to; did he have the self-control to carry that role?

   _____

10. Robinson decided that he did, and the two men shook hands. _____

Van Goor and Hacker, *Developmental Exercises for
The Bedford Handbook,* 9th ed. (Boston: Bedford, 2014)

49-2 | Sentence types   **185**

EXERCISE 49-3 ◆ Sentence types: Review

To read about this topic, see section 49 in *The Bedford Handbook*, Ninth Edition.

Indicate on the blank after each sentence in the following paragraphs whether the sentence is simple (S), compound (C), complex (CX), or compound-complex (CC). One of each kind has been labeled for you.

Robinson very quickly had a chance to test his commitment to nonviolence; on the way to training camp in Florida, he and his bride were bumped from flights and refused service in the coffee shop. ____C____ When they finally got to Florida, they rode a segregated bus to get to Daytona Beach. _____ At training camp, white players stayed in nice hotels and ate in hotel dining rooms; Robinson and other blacks had to find homes or motels in the black community and eat in black restaurants. _____ Robinson kept his temper, diverting his anger into the force with which he handled the ball and bat. _____

The story best remembered about Jackie Robinson is probably the one involving Pee Wee Reese, a southerner on the team. ____S____ Some fans at a Cincinnati game yelled that he should not be playing with a black man, and Reese pretended not to hear. _____ He walked up to Robinson on first base, put a hand on his shoulder, and began a conversation. _____ Later, neither man could remember what they had talked about—but the fans understood Pee Wee's gesture and settled down. ____CC____

In his baseball career, Jackie Robinson broke many records and won many awards. _____ In 1962, he was inducted into the Baseball Hall of Fame—the first African American to be so recognized. _____ He was recognized outside the sports world as well, his top honor being the Presidential Medal of Freedom. _____ Again, what he did off the field was even more important than what he did on it. _____

Today, the Jackie Robinson Foundation provides education and opportunities for young people who, in turn, give back to the community. _____ Since its formation in 1973, it has encouraged and supported thousands of young people who commit to lifelong engagement in their own worlds, who understand the importance of their off-the-field lives. ____CX____

Van Goor and Hacker, *Developmental Exercises for The Bedford Handbook*, 9th ed. (Boston: Bedford, 2014)

Answers to Guided Practice and Preview Exercises

EXERCISE 8-1, page 1

Suggested revision:

Young slave Frederick Douglass enjoyed indulging in his favorite fantasy about slave owners. In his fantasy, everyone conspired against the slave owners. Slaves still in bondage gave no hint of a planned escape. Members of the community never revealed the whereabouts of escaped slaves. Slaves who escaped successfully never talked too much about how they got away. Recaptured slaves told their owners nothing at all. Even some white southerners who sympathized with the slaves gave no information to their slave-owning friends. Douglass enjoyed the final part of his fantasy most. In it, Douglass imagined slave owners as being too afraid to hunt escaping slaves. The owners distrusted their slaves, their enemies, and even their friends.

EXERCISE 9-1, page 5

Suggested revision:

In his own time, one famous sixteenth-century Italian was known only by his given name, Leonardo. Today he is still known by that single name. But then and now, his name suggests many different roles: biologist, botanist, inventor, engineer, strategist, researcher, and artist.

Sixteenth-century Venetian soldiers knew Leonardo as a military strategist. When the Turkish fleet was invading their country, Leonardo suggested conducting surprise underwater attacks and flooding the land that the Turkish army had to cross. Engineers knew him as the man who laid out new canals for the city of Milan. Scientists admired him not only for his precise anatomical drawings but also for his discovery that hardening of the arteries could cause death. To Milan's royal court, Leonardo was the artist who was painting impressive portraits, sculpting a bronze horse memorial to the house of Sforza, and at the same time working on a mural of the Last Supper.

Leonardo saw a three-dimensional *s*-curve in all of nature—the flow of water, the movements of animals, and the flight of birds. We recognize the same *s*-curve today in the spiraling form of DNA. Leonardo invented the wave theory: He saw that grain bending as the wind blew over it and water rippling from a stone dropped into it were the same scientific event. It was as easy for him to see this wave in sound and light as to observe it in fields and streams. The math of his day could not explain all his theories, but twentieth-century scientists showed the world that Leonardo knew what he was talking about.

Leonardo saw very clearly that the powers of nature could be destructive and that human beings could be savage. At the same time, he saw a unity holding all of life's varied parts together, a unity he could express in his art.

Leonardo—it's quite a name!

EXERCISE 10-1, page 9

Suggested revision:

Mary Wollstonecraft, an eighteenth-century writer, may have been England's first feminist. Her entire life reflected her belief in equal rights for women in all areas of their lives: personal, intellectual, and professional.

From childhood, she never had accepted and never would accept the idea that men were superior to women. As a young girl, she knew that her drinking and gambling father deserved less respect than her long-suffering mother did. As an adult, she demanded that society give her the same freedom it gave men.

Wollstonecraft also demanded that men pay attention to her ideas. She did not argue about an idea. Instead, she gave an example of what she objected to and invited her readers to think about it from various points of view. Working this way, she made few enemies among intellectuals. Indeed, she was attracted to and respected by some of the leading intellectuals of her day. Among them she was as well known on one side of the Atlantic as on the other. Thomas Paine, the American orator and writer, probably knew her better than Samuel Johnson, the English writer, did.

Professionally, she was a governess, a teacher, and an author. When her father's drinking destroyed the family, she and her sisters started a girls' school. Eventually, financial problems forced the school to close, but not before Mary had acquired enough firsthand experience to write *Thoughts on the Education of Daughters* (1786). As competent as or more competent than other writers of the day, she was a more persuasive advocate for women than most other writers were.

Modern feminists may find it ironic that current encyclopedia entries for "Wollstonecraft" refer researchers to "Godwin," her married name––where they will find her entry longer than the entry for her famous husband, William Godwin.

EXERCISE 11-1, page 13

Suggested revision:

Sometimes it's hard to separate history from folklore. Casey Jones, John Henry, Johnny Appleseed, Uncle Sam—which of these were real men? We've heard their stories, but are those stories true?

There really was a railroad engineer called Casey Jones; he got that nickname because of Cayce, Kentucky, where he lived as a boy. There really was a Cannonball too; it was the Illinois Central's fast mail and passenger train. There really was a wreck of Engine No. 382, and Casey died while slowing the train to save his passengers. Legend has it that when workers found his body in the wreckage, his hand was still on the air-brake lever. (Air brakes had recently been installed on trains to increase their braking power.)

John Henry was an African American railroad worker of great strength. In legend and song, he died after a timed contest against a steam drill. By using a hammer in each hand, John Henry won the contest. He drilled two holes seven feet deep; the steam drill bored only one nine-foot hole. The real John Henry died on the job, crushed by rocks that fell from the ceiling of a railroad tunnel.

John Chapman, better known as Johnny Appleseed, was a wealthy and well-liked nurseryman who kept moving his place of business west as the frontier moved west. His boyhood friend Sam Wilson supplied meat to the US troops during the War of 1812. A worker told a government inspector that the "US" stamped on the meat stood for "Uncle Sam." Although it was a joke, it caught on, and Congress made the "Uncle Sam" identification official in the 1960s.

EXERCISE 12-1, page 17

Suggested revision:

Hearing the name Karl Marx, people usually think first of Russia. Marx never lived in Russia at all. Actually, he spent almost all of his adult life in England. He was a political exile for the last half of his life.

Marx lived first in Germany. Born of Jewish parents, he completed his university studies with a PhD at the University of Jena. His favorite professor tried to get Marx an appointment to teach at the university. When that professor was fired, Marx gave up hope of teaching at Jena or any other German university. Because he was denied a university position, Marx had to earn his living as a journalist. He worked briefly as a newspaper editor in Germany.

Next came France, Belgium, and a return to Germany. First Marx and his new bride moved to Paris, where Marx worked for a radical journal and became friendly with Friedrich Engels. When the journal ceased publication, Marx moved to Brussels, Belgium, and then back to Cologne, Germany. He did not hold a regular job, so he tried desperately to earn at least enough money to feed his family.

After living in Paris and Brussels, Marx decided he would settle in London. He and his family lived in abject poverty while Marx earned what little income he could by writing for an American newspaper, the *New York Tribune*.

EXERCISE 13-1, page 21

Suggested revision:

Do you know how slavery began in America or how it ended? When the *Mayflower* landed in what is now Massachusetts in September 1620, slaves were already in America. A Dutch ship had unloaded and sold twenty Africans in Jamestown, Virginia, the year before.

Actually, slavery in America began long before that. Many early explorers brought slaves with them to the new land, and some historians claim that one of the men in Christopher Columbus's crew was a slave. From the 1500s to the 1800s, slave ships brought ten million African slaves across the ocean.

Most of the slaves stayed in Latin America and the West Indies, but the southern part of the United States received about 6 percent of them. Few northerners owned slaves, and opposition to slavery was evident by the time of the American Revolution. Rhode Island prohibited the importation of slaves even before the Revolutionary War. After the war, six northern states abolished slavery at once, and other states passed laws to phase out slavery; even Virginia enacted legislation encouraging slave owners to emancipate their slaves.

But it took a war, a tricky political situation, and a very clever former slave to free all slaves. History gives Abraham Lincoln the credit for liberating the slaves during the Civil War, and he deserves some credit, but emancipation was not his idea. Originally, no government officials seriously considered emancipation because they were so focused on winning the war to save the Union. Then an important black man talked to Lincoln and gave him the idea and the reason. This man said that freeing slaves would be good for the war effort and asked if Lincoln would agree to do it. Who was this man? He was Frederick Douglass, fugitive slave and newspaper editor.

EXERCISE 14-1, page 25

Suggested revision:

No one who knew Albert Einstein as a young child would ever have believed that he might one day be called the smartest man in the world. None of his teachers could have predicted success for him. A shy, slow learner, Albert always got into trouble in class. He consistently failed the subjects he did not like. His family could not have predicted his success either. Albert could not even get to meals on time. Night after night his parents had to postpone dinner until servants searched the house and grounds and found the boy. He would be full of apologies but have no explanation to offer for his lateness

except that he was "thinking." Once his angry father dangled his big gold watch at Albert and told him to figure out how late he was. Albert, who could not tell time, was fascinated by the tiny magnetic compass hanging from the watch chain. The boy asked so many questions about the compass that he did not eat much dinner anyway. When Albert begged his father to lend him the compass to sleep with, his father let him borrow it. Years later Einstein wondered whether that little compass had been the beginning of his interest in science.

EXERCISE 15-1, page 29

Suggested revision:

Everyone has heard of Martin Luther King Jr. After studying for the ministry at Boston University and earning a doctorate in theology, he went home to the South to work as a minister. He started working in civil rights and became the most influential leader of that cause in America. When he died, the victim of an assassin's bullet, his name was almost synonymous with "civil rights." Historians and biographers have recorded his leadership in the fight to gain basic civil rights for all Americans. Many people who know of his civil rights work, however, are not aware of his skill as a writer. In addition to his carefully crafted and emotional speeches, King produced other important writing.

Among King's most famous writings is his "Letter from Birmingham Jail." Written to answer a statement published by eight Alabama ministers that King's work was "unwise and untimely," the letter shows King to be a man who had great patience with his critics. Eager to get these ministers to accept his point of view, King reminds them that they are ministers. Their goodwill, he says, should help them see that his views hold value. Instead of attacking them personally, he analyzes their arguments and then presents his own views. Does he use many of the emotional appeals for which he is justly famous? No, in this letter King depends on logic and reasoning as the tools to win his argument.

EXERCISE 16-1, page 33

Suggested revision:

The establishment of the National Park Service was set in motion in 1912 when forty-five-year-old Stephen Mather was hiking in California's Sequoia National Park and met John Muir, the famous wilderness advocate who had founded the Sierra Club. Two years after that influential visit, Mather visited Sequoia and Yosemite and was appalled that the parks were not being maintained properly. When he complained in a letter to Franklin Lane, secretary of the interior in Washington, DC, Lane wrote back: "Dear Steve, If you don't like the way the parks are being run, come on down to Washington and run them yourself."

Stephen Mather responded by going to Washington, DC, and becoming Lane's assistant. In 1916, the National Park Service was established, and Mather became its first director. He believed so strongly in the establishment and preservation of national parks that he paid the salaries of his employees from his own pocket. In addition, he convinced benefactors to purchase land to donate to national parks. He even purchased land on his own and donated it to the National Park Service.

In addition to being a longtime member of the Sierra Club, Stephen Mather had another, more personal motivation to preserve wilderness areas for future generations. Mather suffered from severe bouts of depression, so he often sought out the wilderness for solace.

Following Mather's death on January 22, 1930, many national parks honored him by displaying a plaque that stated: "There will never come an end to the good that he has done."

EXERCISE 17-1, page 38

Suggested revisions:

One of America's most impressive national parks is Grand Canyon National Park in northern Arizona. Established as a national park in 1919, it is now one of America's most popular landmarks. Each year, nearly five million visitors come to the park to see this spectacular and colorful canyon. Ask the park rangers, and they will tell you that the canyon is nearly a mile deep in places and between ten and eighteen miles wide. The canyon was formed over several million years by the flow of the Colorado River. Although it isn't the world's deepest canyon, it is one of the greatest examples of the power of erosion.

Recreational activities are numerous in Grand Canyon National Park. A round-trip hike to the bottom of the canyon is a memorable experience but the steep, rugged trails can be a challenge, even for experienced hikers. Hikers must carry their own water and be prepared for extreme temperatures. Those who prefer not to hike can take a mule tour down into the canyon or enjoy easy and level trails along the rim. Park rangers offer guided walking tours and will answer questions about the park's history, culture, and geology. Just a mile from the Market Plaza is the Yavapai Geology Museum, which displays photographs and exhibits explaining the park's geological history. However visitors spend their time at the Grand Canyon, they can count on breathtaking views.

EXERCISE 18-1, page 43

Suggested revision:

Thousands of years before Yosemite Valley became one of America's most popular national parks, the Miwok and Paiute tribes lived there. They called themselves the Ahwahneechee, after their name for the valley, "Ahwahnee," which means "place of the gaping mouth." In 1851, the Ahwahneechee were evicted from the valley after conflicts with miners during the Gold Rush era. Later, in 1889, the famous naturalist John Muir persuaded Congress to protect the valley's high country from the damage caused by grazing sheep. Thus, in 1890, more than 1,500 square miles became Yosemite National Park, currently one of America's most famous vacation destinations. Most people are familiar with El Capitan, an iconic Yosemite Valley landmark, a nearly vertical granite rock formation that rises about 3,000 feet from the valley floor to its summit. Another widely recognized mountain is Half Dome, whose western face forms a sheer granite wall. Waterfalls, sequoia trees, and clear mountain streams abound, drawing more than 3.5 million visitors annually to this crown jewel of the National Park Service.

EXERCISE 19-1, page 51

Suggested revision:

Four young Englishmen added a word to the world's vocabulary in the 1960s, a word that became synonymous with the 1960s, especially with the music of that time. That word was, of course, "Beatles." The Beatles became the most famous popular musical group of the twentieth century and have held the loyalty of many fans into the present century.

The Beatles were popular in Liverpool, England, and in Hamburg, Germany, before they came to America on tour and became world famous. Liverpool and Hamburg loved the four young men and their music. The Beatles' favorite club was the Cavern in Liverpool, where they hung out together, played day and night, and attracted many fans. A Liverpool disc jockey first called attention to them, and a Liverpool music critic and record store owner became their first manager. The disc jockey called them "fantastic," saying that they had "resurrected original rock 'n' roll." The music critic who became their manager, Brian Epstein, made them shape up as a group. Promoting them, arranging club dates for them, and badgering record companies for them, he was determined to win a recording contract for this exciting new group.

In England, the record buying led to the publicity. In America, the publicity led to the record buying. Everyone wanted copies of the original singles: "Love Me Do," "Please, Please Me," and "From Me to You." In America, audiences made so much noise that no one could hear the music. Crowds of screaming teenagers surrounded the Beatles wherever they

went, determined to touch one or more of these famous music makers. Reporters observing the conduct of fans at Beatles' concerts found that they had to invent a new word to describe the wild, almost insane behavior of the fans. They called it "Beatlemania."

EXERCISE 20-1, page 57

Suggested revision:

Have you ever heard of the Wobblies? Not many people have these days. That's a shame, because they did at least two things for which they should be remembered. They probably saved the labor movement in America, and they definitely gave American folk music some of its most unforgettable songs. No one really knows how they got their nickname, but almost everyone knows a song or two that they inspired.

The Wobblies were the members of the Industrial Workers of the World (IWW), a small but militant coalition of radical labor groups. The Wobblies could not get along with the major union groups of the day; in fact, they alienated most of those groups.

Although the major unions disliked the Wobblies immensely, they learned some valuable lessons from them. The first lesson was to avoid getting involved in politics. If there was one thing the Wobblies hated more than capitalism, it was politics. The Wobblies avoided politics for one good reason: They [or they] believed that political affiliation caused the death of unions. What else did the major unions learn? They learned to deal realistically with workers' problems. Major unions also learned new recruiting techniques from the Wobblies. In addition, they copied the Wobblies in devoting their energy to nuts-and-bolts issues affecting the workers.

The major unions never recognized their debt to the Wobblies, but the debt was still there for historians to see. When historians began to compile the story of the American labor unions, they finally recognized the contributions of the Wobblies.

EXERCISE 21-1, page 64

convey, are, are, are, has, is, seem, enjoy, is, is

EXERCISE 22-1, page 68

Suggested revision:

Everyone has heard of Dorothy and Toto and their tornado "flight" from Kansas to Oz. Everyone also knows that the Oz adventure was pure fantasy and that it ended happily. But another girl from Kansas took real flights all around the real world. Whenever she landed safely after setting one of her many records, everyone rejoiced and sent congratulations to her. When she disappeared on her last flight, the whole world mourned. Not every pilot can claim to have that kind of following.

Neighbors knew that Amelia Earhart would not be a typical "lady." A child as curious, daring, and self-confident as Amelia was bound to stand out from her peers. When she and her sister Muriel were young, girls were supposed to play with dolls. If girls played baseball or collected worms, they were called "tomboys" and were often punished. Boys and girls even had different kinds of sleds—the girls' sleds were lightweight, impossible-to-steer box sleds.

But the Earhart family lived by its own rules. Amelia's father, whom she depended on for approval, bought Amelia the boys' sled she longed for. Many fast trips down steep hills gave Amelia a foretaste of flying with the wind in her face.

The closest Amelia came to flying was on a homemade roller coaster. She and her friends built it, using an old woodshed for the base of the ride. They started eight feet off the ground and tried to sled down the slope without falling off. No one was successful on the first attempt, but Amelia kept trying until she had a successful ride. Satisfied at last, she declared that the ride had felt "just like flying."

EXERCISE 23-1, page 72

Suggested revision:

George and Mary Jones lived in Memphis during the Civil War. They were sympathetic to the Union, but the city definitely favored the Confederates. Being caught in the middle made the war years especially hard on them. They looked forward to a much better life after the war.

At first, it seemed that they were going to have that better life. George got a job as a labor organizer, and Mary stayed at home to care for their four healthy children. Then came yellow fever. In nine months, Mary went from a happy wife and mother to a despondent widow with no children. She had to find work. Because a person must have some meaning for living, she needed work that she could care strongly about.

By 1900, Mary had become involved in union activities all over the United States. She found her calling among the coal miners and their wives, a calling she followed for the next thirty years. Making friends with the workers and outwitting private detectives, she held secret meetings to help the miners organize and plan strategy. The newspaper often reported her ability to outwit and outlast mine bosses and lawyers as well as to reawaken courage in disconsolate workers.

Mary Jones spent many nights in jail, but often her jailers did not know what to do with this attractive gray-haired woman whom the workers called "Mother." The jailers' confusion simply amused Mary, who was far more used to jail than her jailers could imagine.

EXERCISE 24-1, page 76

They, them, We, her, They, them, they, he, president's, she

EXERCISE 25-1, page 80

who, Who, who, whom, who, who

EXERCISE 26-1, page 84

Novelists have often used their storytelling talents to influence people's thinking. Charles Dickens did it in nineteenth-century England. From *David Copperfield* to *Oliver Twist*, book after book depicted the plight of the poor and other really unfortunate members of society. Harriet Beecher Stowe did it in nineteenth-century America, but with hardly as many books. Her *Uncle Tom's Cabin* depicted slavery so well that the book strongly influenced antislavery sentiments in the decade before the Civil War.

Harriet Beecher Stowe considered slavery sinful and wanted her book to help end slavery quickly and peacefully. People first read parts of the novel ten years before the beginning of the war. An abolitionist magazine published the book a few chapters at a time, hoping the effect of the story would make readers feel so bad about slavery that they would rally to the abolitionist cause. Many people, reading *Uncle Tom's Cabin* installment by installment, did become convinced that nothing could be worse than living in slavery on a southern plantation.

None of the abolitionists, who devoted their energy to abolishing slavery, expected a perfect world when the book itself was published in 1852. But they certainly hoped that the book would be influential. It was. Of all the novels published that year, it was the top seller on both sides of the Atlantic. Its popularity was good news for the abolitionists. Harriet Beecher Stowe's wish had come true.

EXERCISE 27-1, page 88

Suggested revision:

Most Americans today don't realize that the American democratic system did not always include African Americans and women. The constitutional amendments passed after the Civil War granted former slaves and all native-born African American men full voting rights, but the new amendments ignored women. Women had to wait much longer—more than half a century—to be given the right to vote.

Some individual states allowed women to vote as early as 1900, but by 1910 women activists decided to focus their energy on a federal amendment. When Woodrow Wilson became president in 1913, women demonstrated along the inauguration route, marching and holding signs demanding the vote for women. Then in 1917, Alice Paul and a militant faction of the suffrage movement picketed the White House and even chained themselves to fences. When they were threatened and attacked by male mobs, police ignored the men and arrested the women. In prison, the women endured filthy cells, force-feeding when they went on a hunger strike, and ill treatment. Some women were restrained for many hours in uncomfortable positions with their arms high over their heads. One angry official repeatedly asked a doctor to declare one or more of the women insane. (The doctor refused.)

President Wilson was a man with major problems—a war abroad and women fighting for their rights at home. At first he tolerated the women picketers; he even sent coffee out to them. Then he just wanted the women to lay down their signs and banners and go home. But the increasing pressure from moderate and radical voices in the movement as well as public outrage over the women's prison treatment finally forced Wilson to support a constitutional amendment for women's voting rights.

EXERCISE 27-5, page 92

Suggested revision:

Almost everyone has heard about Aesop's fables, but most people know very little about Aesop himself. Most of what we know about Aesop is a mixture of hearsay and conjecture. We do know that he was a slave in Greece. One theory is that before he came to Greece he had lived in Ethiopia for most of his life and that "Aesop" is a much-shortened form of "the Ethiopian."

Aesop was not a storyteller then, though he would have loved to speak well enough to tell a good story. He stuttered so badly that he did not even try to talk. In one story we learn, however, that he *could* communicate. A neighbor brought a gift of figs to Aesop's master. Greatly pleased, the master planned to enjoy the figs after his bath and directed that they be put in a cool place until he was ready. While the master was bathing, the overseer and his friends ate the figs. When the master discovered the loss of his figs, the other slaves placed the blame on Aesop. They knew that if Aesop were able to speak, he could defend himself, but they did not fear this stammering slave.

The master ordered that Aesop be flogged, but Aesop got the master to delay punishment briefly. After drinking a glass of warm water, Aesop ran his fingers down his throat and vomited only water. Pointing at the overseer, he made gestures that the overseer and his friends should do as he had done. They drank the water, ran their fingers down their throats—and vomited figs.

Although Aesop's cleverness saved him from a flogging, it also made an enemy of the overseer. Aesop discovered a basic truth about life: Being right doesn't always help one to make friends.

EXERCISE 28-1, page 97

Suggested revision:

Immigrants have come to the United States from all over the world. Initially, new settlers were mostly European, Irish, or English. By the early twentieth century, many Asians had taken a frightening boat trip across the Pacific to get here. Usually the men came first. After they had made enough money for passage, their wives and children were brought over. All thought that if they worked hard, they would make a good life, as earlier European immigrants had done. A large number of Chinese and Japanese settled in the western part of the United States.

These new immigrants worked on the railroads and in the mines. American businesses recruited Chinese labor because American workers would not accept the wages that were paid. Why did workers decide to come to America anyway? Somehow the idea got started that America was a "golden mountain" where people could pick up gold nuggets after an easy climb. Once they got here, most immigrants worked hard because they hoped to make enough money to bring relatives over to America too.

Before and during World War II, many Germans who had been persecuted by Hitler escaped to America. After the war, thousands of "displaced persons" were welcomed by the United States. Later, refugees from Asia, Africa, Latin America, and the Caribbean wanted to be accepted. Franklin D. Roosevelt once said, "All of our people all over the country, except the pure-blooded Indians, are immigrants or descendants of immigrants." If Roosevelt were alive today, he would know that his statement is still true.

EXERCISE 29-1, page 106

Suggested revision:

People all over the world have stories that are part of their culture. Many cultures have a creation story that explains how the world came to be. Sometimes the story tells how a single piece of the world got its characteristics. It is not surprising that these stories exist; what is surprising is how similar the stories are. Consider the Cinderella story, for example. Cinderella has different names in different places, and details of her adventure are not the same; but the basic story echoes around the world.

In Egypt, she is called Rhodopis (the word means "rosy cheeked"). Rhodopis is a Greek slave in an Egyptian home. She does not have eyes or hair like anyone else in the home. Her green eyes look quite different from the eyes of the other girls. Their dark, straight hair almost never gets tangled; her yellow, curly hair blows into a tangled mass around her face. Her light-skinned face turns red and burns when she is in the sun too long. When someone calls her "Rosy Rhodopis," she blushes, and her cheeks become rosier.

Unable to make friends with the other girls, Rhodopis turns to the animals in the nearby woods and streams for companionship.

EXERCISE 30/31-1, page 110

Suggested revision:

A descendant of one of the earliest immigrants to North America played a pivotal role in helping later Americans explore their country. There were tribes of American Indians living all over what is now the United States. Each tribe had its own language and customs. Some tribes raided others and took prisoners who then became the raiding tribes' slaves. That is what happened to a young Shoshone girl now known as Sacagawea.

This girl, like many young girls, had a nickname, "He-toe." "He-toe" was the sound a local bird made, and the girl's movements were as swift as that bird's. When a raiding party of Hidatsas easily captured this young girl, they named her Sacagawea—"bird woman." Sacagawea was about twelve years old. The frightened young girl did not try to escape but accepted her role and worked for her captors. In [or After] a few months, she had acquired a reputation for good sense and good work.

The tribe married Sacagawea to a white man, Toussaint Charbonneau; she was his second wife. Soon pregnant, this typical Indian wife did the chores and left all decisions to her husband; but inwardly, she longed to explore new places and meet new people. She may have been controlled by her husband, but she never missed a chance to learn whatever she could.

When white men appeared, many Indians were curious. Sacagawea had never seen a man with yellow hair—or red hair. Nor had she ever seen a black man. All these men were trying to get to the "Big Water" far to the west. They would have to cross mountains that they had not even seen yet. They needed horses and guides that the Shoshone could supply and an interpreter who could speak the Shoshone language. Imagine their surprise when this interpreter, whom they had hoped to find, turned out to be a woman—an attractive young Shoshone woman.

EXERCISE 32/33-1, page 118

Young adult dystopian literature is a popular genre with a growing fan base worldwide; its books are characterized by degradation, totalitarian states, and dehumanization. With the release of the film version of Suzanne Collins's *The Hunger Games*, the genre has amassed a following similar to that of wizards and vampires in fiction and pop culture. Writers such as Lois Lowry and M. T. Anderson have been producing award-winning dystopian work for years. But the wild popularity of such writers reveals that young readers welcome the serious, dark work being marketed to them. The dystopian novel takes risks, and teenagers like risks. In sophisticated ways that are satisfying to young readers, these books depict pain, loss, and the anxieties of growing up.

Dystopia is the opposite of utopia, which is any system of political or social perfection, an ideal place or state. Dystopia signifies regression. It is a fictional society characterized by poverty, oppression, disease, or overcrowding. The world in a dystopian novel is recognizable as a warped version of our own; people may survive an epic tragedy, often environmental or political, and survivors form a society that curtails freedoms to protect citizens. A hero or heroine must triumph over terrible odds to better the society and restore harmony. The novels are often violent. While the violence may disturb parents, teenagers want stories with weight and intensity. They want to immerse themselves in a world where there is no happy ending, a world that challenges and shocks them and where they can see the best and the worst of humanity.

EXERCISE 34-1, page 127

When Cheryl Toussaint came in second in a race she had never planned to run, she started on a road that led to the Olympics and a world record.

Cheryl began running almost by accident one day when she went to watch a city-sponsored track meet in Brooklyn, New York. During the preliminaries, the officials announced an "open" race; it was one that anyone could enter. Cheryl wanted to enter, but she was dressed in a skirt and sandals. Four things made her run: One [*or* one] friend traded shoes with her, another let her borrow jeans, several called her "chicken" if she didn't run, and one girl dared her to run. Coming in second in that race led this teenager to many places, including Munich, Germany; Toronto, Canada; and Montreal, Canada.

There were, however, many races to run and lessons to learn. Cheryl joined the all-female Atoms Track Club, and she began training under Coach Fred Thompson. Like most coaches, Fred had his own way of testing newcomers. He watched new runners carefully; however, he gave them no special attention. Instead, he just gave them orders one after another. He would tell Cheryl to run laps, perform exercises, and repeat practice starts; at the same time, he would never comment on how she performed. If the newcomers endured the hard, time-consuming workouts without encouragement or praise, Thompson was sure that they were ready for real coaching.

Cheryl quit after two months; for six more months, she stayed away from the club. During that time, she thought about her attitude toward work, her poor record at school, her pleasure in running, and her lack of goals. When she returned to the club, Thompson welcomed her back. Coach Thompson knew how special Cheryl was. He not only convinced her she was college material but also pushed her to achieve the highest goal of the amateur athlete—competing in the Olympics.

EXERCISE 35-1, page 131

In 1951, Althea Gibson broke the color barrier in women's tennis and became admired all over the world. No one who knew her as a teenager would have predicted her success. By the time Althea Gibson reached her teens, her record showed three indications of trouble: running away from home, dropping out of school, and losing the one job she had been able to find. To survive in her neighborhood, Althea depended on a small welfare allowance, occasional handouts, and plain old luck. She listed her skills as the following: good bowler, great two-on-two basketball player, and fast paddleball player. Even after she began playing tennis and moving in upper-class Harlem society, she resented the efforts of the society ladies to improve her. They busied themselves with tasks such as correcting her manners and restricting her behavior. Looking back, she summed up her earlier attitude: She [or she] said she hadn't been ready to study about "how to be a fine lady." At eighteen, she finally got a waitressing job, a congenial roommate, and a good friend.

EXERCISE 36-1, page 135

During the 1990 troubles in Panama, American television and newspaper reporters had an exciting piece of news. They reported that for the first time American female soldiers had been engaged in actual combat. Acting as her soldiers' leader, Captain Linda Bray led her troops into combat. Names of two additional women who were involved in combat, Staff Sergeant April Hanley and Private First Class Christina Proctor, were reported in the newspapers. Theirs were the only names reported, although other women also took part in the fighting.

It wasn't the first time an American woman had fought in an American battle, but it's not likely that many people are aware of that fact. The Civil War had its female fighters too. Loreta Janeta Velazquez fought for the Confederates in the Civil War after her husband's death. Like many other women whose husbands were killed in that war, she must have asked herself, "Who's going to take his place in battle?" The decision to fight was hers alone. Someone is sure to ask how that was possible, especially in those days. Military identification was not very sophisticated in the 1860s. Someone's willingness to fight was that person's major qualification, and each fighting unit needed to replace its losses as fast as possible. Velazquez simply disguised herself in men's clothing, found a troop needing replacements, and joined the fight. Loreta Janeta Velazquez was Linda Bray's Civil War predecessor.

EXERCISE 37-1, page 139

1. The doctor answered, "You can do nothing but pray."
2. When the bandages were removed and the shades were opened to let in the bright sunlight, the doctor asked, "What do you see?"
3. "Nothing," said the boy. "I see nothing."
4. The village priest said, "I have recently seen a remarkable school." He had just returned from a trip to Paris.
5. "In this school," he added, "blind students are taught to read."
6. "You didn't say 'read,' did you?" asked the boy's father.
7. The boy responded to the priest's words as if they were a trick of some kind: "Now you are joking with me. How can such a thing be possible?"
8. The boy, Louis, thought it would be great fun to visit that school someday.
9. His father promised, "We will go soon, Louis."
10. And so it happened that ten-year-old Louis Braille entered the National Institute for Blind Youth and began the long effort to erase the fear people had of even the word "blind." [Or the word *blind* can be italicized, without quotation marks.]

EXERCISE 38-1, page 143

After Louis Braille invented his new system that would allow blind people to read and write, he tested it thoroughly. Students and faculty of the National Institute for Blind Youth were excited at how easily they could master it. They encouraged Louis to demonstrate the system to the French educational authorities, who made the rules for the institute. Louis agreed to do so.

When Louis held the demonstration, all went well. What excitement he and his friends felt! But the authorities would not recommend that the institute adopt Louis's new system. Why didn't the French authorities recognize the advantages of Braille's system? Did they have a vested interest in the old system of teaching the blind? Or a real doubt about the new system? Whatever their reasons, they delayed the pleasures of reading for thousands of people. In addition, a new director, Dr. Pignier, even outlawed the use of the system at the institute for four years.

Although unhappy and disheartened, Braille never gave up; he knew his system would enable the blind to read.

EXERCISE 39-1, page 148

The most famous woman in America is Miss Liberty—a 450,000-pound, 154-foot resident of New York City. For people all over the world, the Statue of Liberty symbolizes America. Yet the idea for the statue came not from America, England, or even New York itself—but from France. Three men can claim credit for the construction of Miss Liberty: (1) Frédéric-Auguste Bartholdi, sculptor; (2) Alexandre-Gustave Eiffel, structural engineer; and (3) Richard Morris Hunt, architect. France gave the statue to the United States, and the United States provided the pedestal on which it stands.

Two Americans contributed significantly to the statue. The first was Joseph Pulitzer, then owner and publisher of the *New York World* and a Russian immigrant. He led several fund-raising efforts and urged every American to give what he or she could to help build the pedestal. The second American who contributed significantly was Emma Lazarus. She wrote the famous lines on the bronze plaque inside the statue. Her three-word title "The New Colossus" (which means "huge statue") alludes to a statue built in the harbor of Rhodes in ancient Greece. The most quoted lines from "The New Colossus" are probably these: "Give me your tired, your poor, / Your huddled masses yearning to breathe free."

EXERCISE 40/41/42-1, page 153

Everyone has heard of Christopher Columbus, but not many people know much about him. Most people learn that he discovered America in AD 1492. Some people know that he had three ships, and they might be able to name them. (The ships were the *Niña*, the *Pinta*, and the *Santa María*.) A few people might even remember that Columbus thought he had found the Indies. And those with great self-confidence might be willing to guess at the number of trips he made to his Indies. (It was four.) Probably no one could tell you his favorite word, *adelante*.

If they were asked what Columbus was trying to prove with his expensive journey, most people would reply that he was trying to prove that the world is round. They would be wrong. If they were asked what Columbus meant by the term *Indies*, they would most likely say "India." They would be wrong again. If they were asked what Columbus's rank was, they would most likely say "captain." They would be wrong again. If they were asked what his sailors feared most, a number of them would reply, "They feared that the boats would fall off the edge of the earth." And they would be wrong again.

Isn't it strange that people can be so ignorant about a well-known man like Columbus?

EXERCISE 43/44/45-1, page 157

Suggested revision:

Columbus's return to Spain from his first exploration was difficult. The *Niña* and the *Pinta* were separated, the *Niña* almost sank, and the governor on the island of Santa María had put Columbus's whole crew in jail. It seemed a miracle that both boats survived their journeys and arrived in the harbor at Palos on the same day.

As difficult as that return was, the reception at court quite made up for it. Columbus certainly made an all-out effort to impress the court, the city, and the entire country. Lavishly attired, he received a grand welcome as he led his entourage into Barcelona, the Spanish capital. It must have been a sight to behold: a procession like none Barcelona had ever seen before. Leading the parade was a gaudily bedecked horse carrying Columbus, followed by six captive "Indians" and all the crew. Everyone but Columbus was carrying boxes, baskets, and cages full of interesting and exotic items.

When the group reached the throne room, King Ferdinand and Queen Isabella stood up to greet Columbus formally and admire his apron-covered captives. Columbus asked the royal couple to accept gifts of plants, shells, darts, thread, and gold. As intrigued as they were with the other gifts, King Ferdinand and Queen Isabella basically wanted the gold. Luckily, Columbus had collected enough of it to satisfy them.

By the end of his first week home, Columbus had such prestige that everyone wanted to accommodate the wishes of the Italian sailor at the court of Spain. Columbus had no doubt that he would receive a commission for a second voyage of exploration or even colonization.

EXERCISE 46-1, page 163

readers, N; are, MV; of, P; its, ADJ *or* PN; and, C; or, C; formal, ADJ; starts, MV; simply, ADV; with, P; should, HV; everyone, PN; about, P; certain, ADJ; when, C; them, PN; acts, MV; government, N; bold, ADJ; been, HV

EXERCISE 47-1, page 172

group, S; had, V; problem, DO; they, S; went, V; They, S; gave, V; paintings, IO; bursts, DO; lovers, S; were surprised, V; artists, S; made, V; scenes, DO; bright, OC; would pour, V; sunshine, S; Were, V; paintings, S; bright, SC; cheerful, SC; painters, S; are admired, V; forms, S; are, V; examples, SC; Both, S; showed, V; viewers, IO; objects, DO

EXERCISE 48-1, page 178

Verbal phrases: bringing the music to American audiences; seeing the rise in popularity; to incorporate house elements in their songs

Prepositional phrases: for bringing the music to American audiences; to American audiences; in Paris; in the 1980s; as a DJ; with French rapper Sidney Duteil; through Europe and the United States; like Madonna; in popularity; in their songs; of massive music festivals like Miami's Winter Music Conference; like Miami's Winter Music Conference; in 2012

Subordinate clauses: who has been called the lord of modern club music; when he worked as a DJ; which was a hip-hop collaboration with French rapper Sidney Duteil; which in 2012 had more than 200,000 attendees

EXERCISE 49-1, page 184

Simple; Complex: Even if they are not sports fans (subordinate clause); Complex: what Jackie Robinson did on the ball field, what he did off the field (subordinate clauses); Compound; Complex: Because the football team was not integrated (subordinate clause); Complex: While he was still in the army—and a second lieutenant to boot (subordinate clause); Simple; Compound-complex: when he refused to go to the back (subordinate clause); Complex: When his case came up (subordinate clause); Complex: that followed (subordinate clause)